D1006815

TEAR DOWN THE WALLS!

A History of the American Civil Rights Movement

TEAR DOWN THE WALLS!

A HISTORY OF THE AMERICAN CIVIL RIGHTS MOVEMENT

by Dorothy Sterling

DOUBLEDAY & COMPANY, INC., GARDEN CITY, NEW YORK

In memory of Martin Luther King, Jr., the latest in the long roll of men and women who have given their lives in the struggle for equality in the United States. Dr. King was assassinated in Memphis, Tennessee, on April 4, 1968.

Acknowledgments

Many thanks are due to the staffs of the National Association for the Advancement of Colored People, the Student Nonviolent Coordinating Committee, the National Urban League, Congress of Racial Equality, Southern Christian Leadership Conference and Southern Conference Educational Fund for their co-operation in supplying information and photographs. I am particularly indebted to the curator and librarians of the Schomburg Collection of the New York Public Library for making available the books, periodicals and illustrations that provided the background for the early chapters of this book.

Very special thanks go to Philip Sterling, not only for going over the manuscript with a careful editorial eye, but for repeatedly suggesting the right phrase and the proper emphasis when I was lost in a maze of facts.

Contents

TEAR DOWN THE WALLS!

A History of the American Civil Rights Movement

"EVERY PERSON OPERATING A BUS LINE
SHALL PROVIDE EQUAL ACCOMMODATIONS . . .
IN SUCH A MANNER AS TO SEPARATE
THE WHITE PEOPLE FROM THE NEGROES . . ."
Section 10, Chapter 6, Code of the City of Montgomery.

CHAPTER 1

Something Happened in Montgomery

Rosa Parks's feet hurt, for good cause. Her job as a seamstress in the Montgomery Fair kept her on the run. All that day of December 1, 1955, she had pinned up hems, raised waistlines, carried dresses back and forth. When the closing time buzzer sounded, she hurried out of the store. Then she boarded a Cleveland Avenue bus, dropped her dime in the box—and hesitated. Where should she sit?

By law and custom, the front rows of seats were reserved for white people. Negroes sat in the back. Halfway up the aisle there was a no man's land where Negroes might sit until the space was needed for white passengers. There were no signs announcing these rules. In Montgomery, the capital city of Alabama, everybody knew them.

But this bus was half empty and Mrs. Parks sank into the first seat behind the "white" section. Her feet began to feel as if they were almost ready to stop hurting. It was a feeling that made it impossible for her to think about anything else. She scarcely noticed that the bus was getting fuller from one stop to the next. Soon all the seats were taken. A few minutes later people were standing in the aisle. White people.

The bus driver, with one eye on his rear-view mirror called, "All right, you niggers, move back!"

The woman next to Mrs. Parks and two men across the aisle rose and silently made their way to the back of the bus. Mrs. Parks sat still. A white man stood beside her, waiting, but she didn't budge.

The bus driver left his wheel and strode up the aisle. "Get up!" he ordered.

Rosa Parks took a deep breath. Suddenly she knew she just— wasn't—going—to—get—up. It wasn't her feet. It was *she* that was tired. She was tired to her very soul of being treated that way.

"No," she said.

"For the last time," the driver roared, "I'm telling you to get up out of that seat."

"No," Mrs. Parks repeated.

The driver slammed out of the bus to call the police. The other passengers stared. All they could see was a small woman whose rimless eyeglasses, tailored suit and hair brushed straight back from her brow made her look like a middle-aged school teacher. They were still staring when she was taken off to jail. Four days later, Rosa Parks, hard-working, churchgoing mother of three, stood before a judge in Montgomery's police court. He fined her ten dollars and costs for disobeying the city's segregation law. That was supposed to be that. It wasn't.

News of her arrest traveled quickly through the Negro community. Every woman who heard of it could not help telling her own story about rude drivers and unfair treatment on the buses. One had been called a "black cow," another a "monkey's cousin" and always the hated word, "nigger." Sometimes, after they paid their fares, the driver ordered Negroes to get off and board the bus again by the back door. While they walked around, he pulled away without them.

The bus-riding insults weren't the worst that Montgomery Negroes lived with, day after day, year after year. Take schools. Colored children went to the Booker T. Washington School—cost, around $200,000—which housed grades one through twelve. Whites had separate elementary and junior high schools, as well as a brand-new Robert E. Lee High School—cost,

Rosa Parks

2milliom

$2,000,000. The Booker T. Washington School overlooked the street and had no outdoor playgrounds. Robert E. Lee was surrounded by rolling lawns, football and baseball fields, "and inside, libraries and laboratories that our kids can only dream of."

Take parks. Washington Park, for Negroes, contained a wading pool, a basketball court and a barbecue pit located only a few yards away from an outdoor toilet. Oak Park, for whites, had a swimming pool, tennis courts, picnic areas, band concerts and a zoo.

Take jobs, housing, voting . . . But there was no need to go all the way down the list. The women at their telephones on that December night had lived with inequity all their lives. When Rosa Parks's cup of humiliation ran over, so did theirs. By morning of December 2 all telephones in the Negro community were buzzing with a new word . . . boycott. "We must stay off the buses to protest Mrs. Parks's arrest . . . Let's stay off the buses until the white folks understand we won't put up with this kind of treatment any longer."

That evening forty men and women met in the Dexter Avenue Baptist Church. A boycott was quickly decided on. No Negro was to ride a bus on Monday, December 5, the day that Mrs. Parks came to trial. But how would people get to work? How long should the boycott last? And most important, how could they inform Montgomery's fifty thousand Negro citizens of their plan?

Before the meeting was over, committees were at work. Negro ministers promised to announce the protest from their pulpits on Sunday. Negro taxi companies agreed to carry workers to their jobs on Monday for the regular ten-cent bus fare. And all day Saturday an army of volunteers fanned out through the Negro neighborhoods, thrusting mimeographed notices of the boycott into outstretched hands. Their leaflet, which was to become a historic document, said simply:

> *Don't ride the bus to work, to town, to school, or any place Monday, December 5.*
>
> *Another Negro woman has been arrested and put in jail because she refused to give up her bus seat.*
>
> *Don't ride the buses to work, to town, to school, or anywhere on Monday. If you work, take a cab, or share a ride, or walk.*
>
> *Come to a mass meeting, Monday at 7:00 P.M., at the Holt Street Baptist Church for further instruction.*

So far, so good. But with the boycott only a day away, the footsore volunteers were afraid that many bus riders had not been reached. A white woman unwittingly came to their aid.

Alarmed when she saw a copy of the leaflet, she telephoned the Montgomery *Advertiser*.

"You should let your readers know what those Negroes are up to," she said.

The newspaper obliged with a front-page story—and every Negro in the city got the message.

Rosa Parks, out on bail, rose early on the morning of December 5. Would the boycott be a success? Montgomery Negroes had been silent for so long that she wondered whether they had the courage to protest now. From her window she watched the first bus go by. Usually it was crowded with domestic workers on their way to white homes across town.

It was empty! So was the second when it passed fifteen minutes later. And the third. All that day Montgomery's dark-skinned citizens walked, thumbed rides, rode in taxis and private cars. Horse-drawn buggies rattled down the streets and more than one man jogged to work on the back of a mule.

Long before seven that evening the Holt Street Baptist Church was jammed with people. Thousands more waited outside, listening to the proceedings through loud-speakers. When Rosa Parks was introduced from the rostrum the audience rose to its feet and cheered.

"We are tired," said Martin Luther King, Jr., the 26-year-old minister of the Dexter Avenue Church. "Tired of being segregated and humiliated, tired of being kicked about by the brutal feet of oppression. We have no alternative but to protest.

"If you will protest courageously, and yet with dignity and Christian love, when the history books are written in future generations, the historians will have to say, 'There lived a great people—a black people—who injected new meaning and dignity into the veins of civilization.' This is our challenge and our overwhelming responsibility."

His listeners accepted the challenge. Forming the Montgomery Improvement Association with Dr. King as president, they voted to continue the bus boycott until their demands were met.

These first demands were modest. "We'd have settled for so

little," a boycott leader said. "A guarantee of courtesy by the bus drivers; seating on a first-come, first-served but still segregated basis; and some Negro drivers."

"We cannot change the seating arrangements," a bus company official replied. "And we have no intention now or in the foreseeable future of hiring 'niggras!'"

The mayor nodded agreement. "Comes the first rainy day and the Negroes will be back in the buses," he said.

It rained—and the buses were empty. Christmas passed and the Negroes walked. When taxi companies were forbidden to cut their rates, the Montgomery Improvement Association set up car pools. Housewives manned telephones and businessmen acted as dispatchers until a fleet of cars—jalopies and Cadillacs—crisscrossed the city. Almost a hundred pickup stations were located in different parts of town so that workers could get rides to and from their jobs.

"What's happened to the colored?" white Montgomery asked. "Looks like all of them have gone crazy or been riled up by agitators."

"Funny thing" a domestic worker laughed. "Our white families say to us it's such a terrible thing that a man like that Reverend King gets the colored people all stirred up, and we say, 'No, ma'am, the Reverend he didn't stir us up, we've been stirred up a mighty long time.' But our white folks, they just don't seem to hear us."

In January, when the bus company's income had been cut by two thirds, the mayor went on television to announce a "get-tough" policy. Negroes, including Rosa Parks, lost their jobs. Their accounts at stores suddenly became due. Car-pool drivers were arrested for every imaginable traffic violation and some that no one had ever heard of before.

On January 26, Dr. King was jailed for driving thirty miles an hour in a twenty-five-mile-an-hour zone. On January 30, his home was bombed. Two days later sticks of dynamite were thrown at the home of another MIA leader. On February 22, ninety-three members of the Improvement Association were arrested, charged with conspiring to conduct an illegal boycott.

The Montgomery movement had been turned down when they tried to buy space in newspapers or radio and television time. Now the arrests and bombings brought the press of the nation to Montgomery. When reporters described "the walking city" and the "miracle of organization" represented by the car pools, contributions poured in from New York and Chicago, Paris and Tokyo. The contributions enabled the MIA to buy station wagons and hire full-time drivers and dispatchers. When local companies canceled their car policies, they bought insurance from Lloyd's of London.

All that spring and summer, the Negroes of Montgomery walked or pooled rides. Their protest gave them a new feeling of dignity.

"Get in, grandma," a pool driver called as he passed an elderly woman who was struggling along with an armful of bundles.

She shook her head. "I'm not walking for myself. I'm walking for my children and grandchildren." And she waved him on.

With this new sense of their own strength, their demands changed. They were no longer willing to settle for the back of the bus and a promise of courtesy. In May they filed a suit in federal court. Six months later they had their answer. The Supreme Court ruled that Alabama's bus segregation laws violated the U. S. Constitution.

"Praise the Lord," one boycotter shouted. "God Almighty has spoken from Washington, D.C."

On December 21, 1956, Negroes boarded the buses of Montgomery again. They sat in any empty seats, front or back, and whites sat with them. For a few weeks there was violence. A sniper fired a bullet into a bus, wounding a woman. Negro homes and churches were bombed.

Then Montgomery faded from the front pages of newspapers and there were bus boycotts in Florida, South Carolina, Louisiana. Negro children went to school in Little Rock while soldiers patrolled the classrooms. Negroes claimed the right to eat at a lunch counter in North Carolina, to borrow books from a Georgia library, to vote in Mississippi. They organized sit-ins, swim-ins, pray-ins, freedom rides. They marched peacefully in Washington and Selma and they rioted in Los Angeles and New York.

Rosa Parks's soft "no" sparked a movement that has spread from coast to coast. It started in Montgomery, but its roots go far back in our history.

"THESE STATES ARE THE AMPLEST POEM,
HERE IS NOT MERELY A NATION BUT
A TEEMING NATION OF NATIONS."

Walt Whitman

CHAPTER 2

Welcome, White Men!

The First Americans

On a windy March day in 1621, a tall copper-skinned man strode from the forest. The Plymouth colonists watched in alarm as he walked toward them.

"Welcome, white men!" he said.

Samoset, the Indian, was welcoming the strangers to his land. He had learned a few words of English from fishermen along the coast. He returned a week later, bringing Massasoit, chief of his tribe. After an exchange of gifts, the white men and Indians drew up a peace treaty.

In those first hard years at Plymouth, the Indians were good neighbors. They introduced the English to American ways of hunting and fishing. They showed them how to plant corn in hills, using herring for fertilizer; how to trap beaver and bake the clams that were so plentiful along the shore. When the Pilgrims celebrated their first Thanksgiving, Massasoit and his men contributed five deer to the feast.

But peace between the two peoples was short-lived. Each year boatloads of Europeans arrived. They settled Boston and Salem and followed Indian trails through the wilderness of Connecticut and Rhode Island. Each year there was less corn land and fewer deer for the Indians. By 1675 King Philip, the son

King Philip

of Massasoit, concluded that the only hope for his people was to say, "White men, go home!"

He said it with guns and the white men answered with an army that wiped out the Indian villages. Those who survived were driven from their homes or sold into slavery in the West Indies. For a long time afterward, King Philip's head hung from a pole, looking down on the settlers of Plymouth. The gun that killed him is still on exhibition in the city's Pilgrim museum.

A million Indians lived on the American continent north of Mexico at the time of Columbus. They were not all one people. Some built stone houses, four and five stories high. Others lived in long log homes or bark-covered tepees. Speaking five hundred different languages, they were as different from each other as Arabs are from Englishmen. But to European eyes, their copper skins and their ignorance of Christianity made them all "savages." When Samoset told his English friends that the Plymouth Indians had been killed by a mysterious plague four years earlier, they saw the plague as the work of God. "By this means Christ, whose great and glorious works are all for the benefit of his churches and his chosen, not only made room for his people to plant, but also tamed the hearts of the barbarous Indians," one Pilgrim wrote in his journal.

With some exceptions, the Europeans' solution of the "Indian question" was a simple one: "The only good Indian is a dead Indian." They died of gunshot wounds and the white man's diseases. Or they packed their few belongings and moved westward until there was no place on the vast continent left for them to go. Today there are fewer than half a million of these "vanishing Americans" in the United States, most of them crowded together on reservations. They did not become citizens of their land, nor were they allowed to vote in national elections until 1924.

Whence Came All These People?

As the first Americans were vanishing, a new breed took their place. One hundred years after King Philip's War, J. Hector St. John de Crèvecoeur, a French immigrant, wrote an enthusiastic account of his neighbors titled "What Is an American?"

"Whence came all these people?" he asked. "They are a mixture of English, Scotch, Irish, French, Dutch, Germans, and Swedes. In this great American asylum, the poor of Europe have met together. Here individuals of all nations are melted into a new race of men.

"How is this accomplished in that crowd of low, indigent people who flock here every year from all parts of Europe? Let me select one as an epitome [example] of the rest. He is hired. He goes to work and works moderately. Instead of being employed by a haughty person he finds himself with his equal, placed at the substantial table of the farmer. If he behaves with propriety, he becomes as it were a member of the family. He now feels himself a man, because he is treated as such.

"If he is wise he spends two or three years in which time he acquires knowledge, the use of tools, the modes of working the lands, felling trees, etc. He purchases some land. His good name procures him credit. He is now possessed of the deed, conveying to him and his posterity 200 acres of land. He is naturalized. His name is enrolled with those of the other citizens of the province. For the first time in his life he counts for something, for hitherto he has been a cypher. From nothing to start into being; from a servant to the rank of a master; from being the slave of some despotic prince, to become a free man, invested with lands. What a change indeed! It is in that change that he becomes an American.

"After a foreigner is arrived, let him listen to the voice of our great parent, which says to him, 'Welcome to my shores, distressed European. Bless the hour in which thou didst see my verdant fields, my fair navigable rivers, and my green mountains! If thou wilt work, I have bread for thee. I will give thee fields to feed and clothe thee; a comfortable fireside to sit by; and a decent bed to repose on. I shall endow thee beside with the immunities of a free man. Go thou and work and till. Thou shalt prosper!"

De Crèvecoeur's picture of his new home was a rosy one. Many Europeans who flocked to America in the 1700s were too poor even to pay their passage money. They sold themselves to ship captains or labor agents, agreeing to work for a certain number of years. Newspapers of the day reported:

". . . There is just arrived from Scotland, a parcel of choice Scotch Servants; Taylors, Weavers, Shoemakers and ploughmen, some for five and others for seven years. . . . Just arrived from London the ship Providence, Capt. Jonathan Clarke, a parcel of very likely servants, mostly Tradesmen, to be sold on reasonable Terms . . . Capt. Hasselwood has arrived from Holland with the latest ship that brought Germans. It is the fourteenth that has come laden with Germans this year. Besides these 1,000 servants and passengers arrived from Ireland and England."

When an immigrant ship reached port, merchants and farmers came aboard to inspect the cargo. Sometimes the servants were bought in wholesale lots by "soul-drivers" who marched them through the countryside until they were resold. The servants worked hard and they seldom ate at their masters' tables. They had few rights under the law. They were not allowed to marry or to leave their jobs even for an hour without permission, and if they tried to escape, their term of service could be lengthened.

However, when their service came to an end they walked off as free men, often with a new suit of clothes and a pound or two to jingle in their pockets. Some, their spirit broken by the years of servitude, drifted from town to town, never rising above the level of "poor whites." Others, like de Crèvecoeur's farmer, headed for the backwoods where there was land to be had by anyone strong enough to swing an ax.

The Promised Land

The settlers in the new land wrote to their families back home. In Irish peasant huts and German workers' cottages people gathered to hear the "America letters."

> *There is a great many ill conveniences here but no empty bellies.*
> *This is a good country for them that is able to work.*
> *Wages here are three times as high as in the old country.*
> *Even on week days we eat wheat bread.*
> *Here everyone is equal. The teacher and the cobbler, they have the same title—Mister.*
> *Schools are free for everyone, Jew and Gentile, girl and boy.*

Perhaps the new American boasted a little. Never mind. Times were bad in Europe. Between 1750 and 1850 its population almost doubled. Food was scarce, land prices high. These letters gave hope to the hopeless.

At first only the young, or those with a little money, left the old country. Then the bad times grew worse. In Ireland families

lived on the yield of an acre planted to potatoes—until a blight
struck the fields and the potatoes turned black and rotten overnight. People roamed the woods hunting berries and wild
roots. An army of living skeletons lined the roads.

"For God's sake, don't let us die of hunger," a farmer begged
a relative across the sea.

Meetings and "donation parties" for starving Ireland were
held in towns all over the United States. From their small
savings the Irish in America scraped together passage money for
their families. "I work on a Railway at 8 shillings per day. I
will be able to pay yours passage withe the help of God on the
First August next. You will be shortly in the lands of Promise,"
a man wrote to his "dear and loveing wife."

A million Irish died of famine in the years between 1846
and 1849 and a million fled to America. A million more migrated
to the United States in the ten years that followed, and another
two million in the next fifty years.

They traveled in the holds of ships, father, mother and children sleeping together in bunks ten feet wide. The cabins were airless, the food bad, the voyage long. One in ten died during the crossing.

For those who survived there came at last the cry of "Land ho!" Clothes and babies were scrubbed, belongings packed and families rushed to the deck for their first glimpse of the New World.

"It's America!" they shouted. "Praise be to God and all the Holy Saints."

The wave of newcomers was trapped in the port cities. By the 1850s the frontier, where land was free, was farther west. It took money and know-how to get there and the Irish peasants had neither. Most could not read or write and some spoke only Gaelic.

They stayed in Boston and New York, crowding into cellars and alleys near the waterfront. Often a hundred people squeezed into a single three-story house. Typhus and cholera broke out, crime rates soared and men tried to drown their misery in the grogshop at the corner.

But there was plenty of work for the able-bodied. Contractors carried gangs of men outside the cities. For wages of a dollar a day, the Irish dug canals, built railroads, paved the highways that were beginning to cross the continent. When they put down their picks and shovels to exchange them for jobs in factories, other work-hardened hands picked them up.

The potato blight had crossed the Irish Sea to the heart of Europe. Hunger and political unrest drove six million Germans to the New World. Two million people came from Norway and Sweden, heading for *framtidslandet*—the land of the future. A cholera epidemic in 1887 set almost five million Italians in motion. Eight million people traveled from eastern Europe— Jews and Russians fleeing Czarist oppression, Poles, Hungarians, Czechs. And from Greece, Albania, Syria, Armenia came three million more, all ragged, unlearned, hungry. By the beginning of the twentieth century thirty-five million Europeans had left their homes for the "promised land" across the sea.

The Melting Pot

Germans and Scandinavians with skills and small savings
followed the Erie Canal to the west. They became homesteaders on the frontiers of Kansas, Minnesota, Wisconsin.
But most of the newcomers, bringing only the clothes on their
backs, could not escape from the Atlantic seaboard. Packed into
barracklike buildings in city slums, they formed Little Italys,
Jewtowns, Polack Alleys. They had their own churches, mutual
aid societies, *landsmannschaften* (Old Country clubs) and they
worked at the hardest jobs for the lowest pay. Italians peddled
ice, mended shoes, laid bricks. Jews bent over sewing machines
in the growing garment industry. Poles and Hungarians drifted
to the coal mines and steel mills. And on the West Coast a
growing number of Chinese dug ditches, harvested crops and
laid railroad ties.

As each new wave of foreigners arrived, the Got-Here-Firsts
looked down on the latecomers. In 1748 young George Washington, the great-grandson of immigrants, was working as a
surveyor in the Blue Ridge Mountains. Meeting a party of
German settlers he noted in his journal that they were "ignorante . . . they would never speak English but when spoken to
they speak all Dutch."

A hundred years later it was the Irish who were "ignorante."
Nicknamed "Paddies" after their patron saint, St. Patrick, they
were "wild . . . drunken . . . roughnecks," so often in trouble
with the law that the police cars that carry prisoners to jail
are still called "paddy wagons." Signs saying NO IRISH
NEED APPLY were posted at factory gates and Irishmen were
denounced as "cheap imported labour who will work for what
Americans cannot live on." Because most Irishmen were Catholics they were criticized for "owing allegiance to the Pope
of Rome."

Later immigrants were called "the refuse of Europe." "A dirty
Irishman is bad enough, but he's nothing comparable to a nasty

Italian loafer," a New Yorker said. "The lowest Irish are far above the level of these creatures." "You don't call an Italian a white man?" a construction foreman was asked. "No sir," he answered. "An Italian is a Dago." To "Dagos" were added "Kikes . . . Polacks . . . Hunkies . . . Chinks."

In California in 1877 an Irish immigrant organized the Workingman's Party. Claiming "America for the Americans," he campaigned against the "Yellow Peril" represented by the Chinese and the "bandy-legged, slant-eyed Japs" in his adopted state. In Iowa ten years later the son of a German immigrant used the same slogan to found the American Protective Association, a secret organization whose members were pledged never to vote for or employ Catholics. In New Orleans in 1891 a mob killed eleven Italians suspected of a crime. In New Jersey in the same year mill workers rioted for three days when fourteen Russian Jews were hired.

Each national group struggled to become accepted. "My father found occasion to instruct or correct us even on the way from the pier," Mary Antin, a thirteen-year-old Jewish immigrant, remembered. "He told us not to lean out of the windows, not to point, and explained the word 'greenhorn.' We did not want to be greenhorns. A fairy godmother to us children led us to a wonderful country called uptown where in a dazzlingly beautiful palace called a department store we exchanged our hateful homemade European costumes which pointed us out as greenhorns for real American machine-made garments."

After five years in the new country, the foreigners could become citizens. With citizenship papers in their pockets, they were the equal of any man—at least on Election Day. In the big cities the immigrant vote often decided an election. Irishmen "fresh from the bogs," Poles who spoke no English, Italians who had to be shown how to hold a pencil to mark their ballots were marched to the polls by local politicians. Before long the new citizens discovered the power that their numbers gave them and began to play the game of politics themselves. An Irishman was elected mayor of New York in 1880, in Boston in 1885. Even today a political ticket in New York is not considered properly balanced unless it includes an Irishman, an Italian and a Jew.*

And then there were the children. "On our second day," Mary Antin wrote, "a little girl from across the alley came and offered to conduct us to school. This child who had never seen us till yesterday, who could not pronouce our names, was able to offer us the freedom of the schools of Boston. No applications made, no questions asked, no examinations, rulings, exclusions. The doors stood open for every one of us."

The greenhorn children who entered school in September knowing only a few words of English were reciting verses in honor of Washington and Lincoln by February. In school they learned that any American boy could become President of the United States. At home they became interpreters to their parents. "My teacher says . . ." Papa, peddling ice on the street, and Mama, scrubbing clothes in the kitchen, began to dream of "my son, the lawyer," "my daughter, the teacher."

The children grew taller and sturdier than their parents. In a generation or two they became lawyers, doctors, teachers, businessmen. As they moved from the crowded Little Italys and Polack Alleys they shortened their foreign-sounding names, changing Kurcyusz to Curtis, Riccio to Rich, Björkegren to Burke. The old country was still remembered on St. Patrick's Day, Columbus Day, Pilsudski Day. But as the paraders marched through the streets, onlookers could no longer tell the Got-Here-Firsts from the Came-Laters. They were all Americans.

This has been the experience of all the immigrant groups that make up our "teeming Nation of nations."

Except for the Negroes.

* And, in recent years, a Negro.

"O, YE CHRISTIANS!
LEARNED YOU THIS FROM YOUR GOD, WHO
SAYS UNTO YOU, DO UNTO ALL MEN AS YOU
WOULD MEN SHOULD DO UNTO YOU? IS IT
NOT ENOUGH THAT WE ARE TORN FROM OUR
COUNTRY AND FRIENDS, TO TOIL FOR YOUR
LUXURY AND LUST OF GAIN? MUST EVERY
TENDER FEELING BE LIKEWISE SACRIFICED?"

Olauda Equiano, an African

CHAPTER 3

Trading in Men

A Numbness Upon the Heart

When Columbus landed on San Salvador in October 1492, the inhabitants of the island came down to the shore to greet him. "I gave them red caps, and glass beads to put round their necks, and many other things of little value, which made them so much our friends that it was a marvel to see," he wrote. "These people are very gentle, being without arms. They should be good servants."

The gentle people of the island did not make good servants. They died of overwork and harsh treatment. In 1517, Bartolomé de Las Casas, the first priest to be ordained in the New World, petitioned the Spanish King in behalf of the Indians. "Consider," he wrote, "whether this hard usage of the poor creatures be consistent with the precepts which God commanded concerning charity to our neighbors." Since the Spaniards needed laborers to work in the mines and on the rice plantations, he suggested that Negroes be imported from Africa instead.

Thus, in the name of charity, the African slave trade to the

Americas began. It lasted for more than three hundred and fifty years. Ten million, fifteen million, perhaps twenty million men, women and children were taken from their homes and brought across the sea in chains. It was the largest and cruelest forced migration in history.

Like the Indians, the Africans were not one people. They were Berber and Bantu, Basuto, Ibo, Koromanti. And Ashanti, Mandingo and Yoruba. They were city dwellers and farmers, herdsmen and hunters, ironworkers and weavers, warriors and poets. Some were as tall as the seven-foot Watusi, whose descendants can be seen on our basketball courts today. Others were as short as the Pygmies who still hunt in their native forests. Their skin colors ranged from yellow-brown to blue-black and they spoke a thousand different languages and dialects.

Columbus lands in the New World

THE

INTERESTING NARRATIVE

OF

THE LIFE

OF

OLAUDAH EQUIANO,

OR

GUSTAVUS VASSA,

THE AFRICAN.

WRITTEN BY HIMSELF.

VOL I.

Behold. God is my falvation : I will truft and not
be afraid, for the Lord Jehovah is my ftrength
and my fong : he alfo is become my falvation.
And in that day fha't ye fay, Praife the Lord, call
upon his name, declare his doings among the people,
Ifaiah xii. 2, 4·

FIRST AMERICAN EDITION.

NEW-YORK:

PRINTED and Sold BY W. DURELL, at his
Book Store and Printing-Office, No. 19, Q. Street,
M,DCC,XCI.

Olaudah Equiano

OR

GUSTAVUS VASSA

the African

White men from Europe and America saw them all as *Negro,* the Spanish word for black. They sailed away with the youngest and strongest. Whole villages were emptied. Tools left behind rusted in the tropical rains and vines from the jungle overran the cities. The slave trade made the "dark continent" dark. It set African civilization back hundreds of years.

Africans were brutalized by the slave trade—and so were the Europeans. Profits from the trade were so great that one slave-ship captain wrote, "It renders those who are engaged in it too indifferent to the sufferings of their fellow creatures. It gradually brings a numbness upon the heart."

The Boy from Benin

Olauda Equiano had never listened to an "America letter." Born in the kingdom of Benin in 1745, he was the son of a village elder. Benin (in what is now Nigeria) was a prosperous

Benin bronze head

city-state. Most of its people were farmers, working their land in common. In the capital where the king lived, there were skilled craftsmen who carved ivory and cast fine statues in bronze. Olauda played in the fields with the other children, dreaming perhaps of someday seeing the king's palace and the famed bronzes of Benin.

When he was eleven, two strangers kidnaped him. They put a gag in his mouth so that his parents couldn't hear him shout, and they carried him off into the jungle. After months of traveling on foot and by canoe, he was delivered to a "factory" on the coast for processing.

These factories were armed fortresses built by companies from different European nations. There Africans were herded into pens and examined by doctors who weeded out the weak and sickly. Each was "marked on the breast with a red-hot iron, imprinting the mark of the French, English or Dutch companies," a trader said. "Care is taken that the women, as tenderest, be not burnt too hard."

The captives were then marched to the beach where the slave ships rocked at anchor. The boy from Benin was terrified by the white men who carried him aboard a ship. "I was persuaded that I had gotten into a world of bad spirits and that they were going to kill me," he wrote many years later. "Their complexions differing so much from ours, their long hair, and the language they spoke (which was very different from any I had ever heard) united to confirm me in this belief. When I looked round the ship and saw a large furnace or copper boiling and a multitude of black people chained together, I no longer doubted of my fate. Quite overpowered with horror and anguish, I fainted. When I recovered, I found some black people about me. I asked them if I were not to be eaten by those white men with horrible looks, red faces, and long hair. They told me I was not. They gave me to understand we were to be carried to these white people's country to work for them.

"I was soon put down under the decks, and there I received such a salutation in my nostrils as I had never experienced in my life. With the loathsomeness of the stench and crying together, I became so sick and low that I was not able to eat, nor had I the least desire to taste anything.

"I now wished for the last friend, death, to relieve me. Soon two of the white men offered me eatables; and, on my refusing to eat, one of them held me fast by the hands, while the other flogged me severely."

Olauda was lucky. Because he was so young he was only put in the hold for short periods. "The closeness of the place, which was so crowded that each had scarcely room to turn himself, almost suffocated us," he wrote. "The shrieks of the women and the groans of the dying, rendered the whole a scene of horror almost inconceivable."

In the early days of the slave trade, captains of the slave ships were divided between "loose packers" and "tight packers." The loose packers argued that if the Africans were given better quarters, more would survive. The tight packers replied that it was a simple matter of shillings and pence. Hundreds were sure to die anyway so that the larger the cargo they started with, the larger their profits would be.

By Olauda's time, the tight packers had won the argument. Using diagrams of their ships (see page 26) they worked out the most efficient ways of stowing their cargo. Each adult was allotted a space sixteen *inches* wide. A boy was allowed fourteen inches, a girl twelve inches. Chained at wrists and ankles, this was the way they traveled for the three weeks to three months that the voyage lasted. "They had not so much room as a man in his coffin," a ship's doctor said. Sometimes five out of ten died during the crossing.

Numbers of these deaths were suicides. Brought up on deck for air, half-crazed men leaped overboard. Others refused to eat. So many went on hunger strikes that the ships carried a special device called, in the best Latin of the day, a *speculum oris*—mouth opener. The device forced open the lips of the captive so that food could be poured into his mouth through a funnel. Still others died of what the ship's doctors named "fixed melancholy." Cut off from home, family, friends —everything that made life worth living—they seemed to "will themselves dead."

For those like Olauda who survived, there came at last the sight of land—"at which the whites on board gave a great shout, and made many signs of joy," he wrote. "We did not know what to think."

When the ship docked, no relatives came to welcome the greenhorns from Africa. Instead "many merchants and planters came on board. They put us in separate parcels and examined us attentively. They also made us jump, and pointed to the land, signifying we were to go there. We thought by this we should be eaten by these ugly men and there was much dread and trembling," Olauda reported.

Once again, he was lucky. Over a period of years, he was sold from master to master—first to a Virginia planter, then to a British naval officer and finally to a Philadelphia merchant who allowed him to buy his freedom. Learning to read and write English, he wrote *The Interesting Narrative of the Life of Olauda Equiano* which sold widely in England and the United States. After its publication in 1789, he spent the rest of his life speaking, writing and petitioning for the end of the slave trade.

The Wild Ones

In the early years of American slavery the kidnaped Africans were brought to the West Indies for "seasoning." Like wild horses being broken to the bridle, they were trained to their new way of life. With whip in hand, a slave driver taught them to rise at daybreak when the conch shell blew, to use a long-handled European hoe instead of the shorter African one and to stand at attention in the presence of a white man.

Many of the Africans died during the seasoning period. Others, made of stronger stuff, survived. Their "fixed melancholy" disappeared and they recovered their willingness to live. Because they were still men, in spite of their chains, their will to live became a will to live free.

The West Indian planters knew this. Far outnumbered by their slaves they lived in fear of rebellions. "In the Negroes we possess a formidable domestic enemy," a Frenchman in the West Indies wrote. "A colony of slaves is a city under constant threat of assault. There one walks on barrels of powder," another added.

To keep the slaves under control they built forts bristling with cannon and imported regiments of soldiers from Europe. Slaves suspected of being rebels were put to death in the cruelest possible way—"by nailing them down on the ground and then applying Fire by degrees from the Feet and Hands, burning them gradually up to the head, whereby their pains are extravagant," an Englishman reported. "For Crimes of a lesser nature they are whipped till they are Raw. Some put on

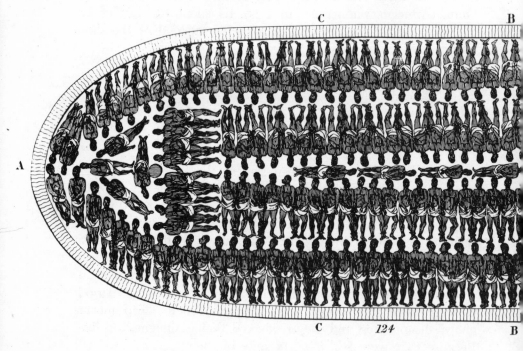

Slave ship

their Skins Pepper and Salt to make them smart, at other times
their Masters will drop melted Wax on their Skins and use
several exquisite Torments. These punishments are sometimes
merited by the Blacks who are a very perverse Generation of
People."

Despite these displays of white might, the Africans fought
to free themselves. Five years after Las Casas' fateful petition
to the king, the slaves of Haiti, then a Spanish possession,
rebelled. This was followed by a second rebellion and a third,
a fourth, a fifth until the Caribbean islands and nearby South
America were in a constant state of warfare.

In Brazil and Dutch Guiana, runaways built villages in the
dense forests. The Republic of Palmares, a Negro state in
northern Brazil lasted for sixty years, falling only when an

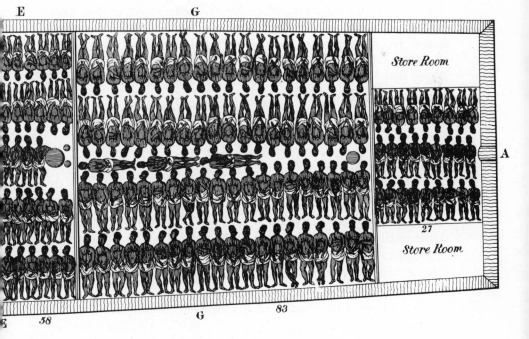

army of seven thousand Portuguese soldiers marched against it. The settlements in Dutch Guiana were never conquered. In 1825, after almost two centuries of fighting, the government signed a formal treaty of peace with the Negroes. Today there are still villages in Dutch Guiana whose people live as their African ancestors did in the days of the slave trade.

In the mountains of Jamaica, Cuba, Haiti, bands of black men, often a thousand strong, lived as outlaws. At night they raided the plantations, running off with food and slaves. The members of these guerrilla bands were called maroons—the wild ones—after the Spanish word *cimarrón* which means "wild, untamed."

The first African slaves to reach the United States mainland came in 1526 when a party of Spaniards brought a hundred slaves to what is now South Carolina. Their colony was short-lived. In less than six months, the slaves rebelled, killing their masters. When the surviving Spaniards fled to Haiti, the slaves joined forces with the Indians and lived as free men. These black men from Africa were the real Got-Here-Firsts for they made their home in the United States-to-be almost a century before the landing of the Mayflower.

Perpetual Servants

Although Africans were brought to Spanish Florida in the sixteenth century, the slave trade to the English colonies did not begin until 1619. It started slowly. Twenty Negroes were landed at Jamestown, Virginia, eleven at New York. A cargo of salt, tobacco and slaves was unloaded in Boston. Other black men trickled into Pennsylvania, New Jersey, Maryland.

At first they were treated as if they were indentured servants like the men and women who came from Europe. They worked alongside the Scottish and Irish, living with them, eating with them, and escaping when they did. "Run away in April," an advertisement in a Philadelphia newspaper said. "A Mulatto slave Named Richard Molson of Middle Statue, about forty years old. He is in company with a White Woman Named Mary who is supposed now goes for his wife. Whoever shall apprehend the said Fugitives shall be well rewarded."

Before long, however, a New Englander was writing, "I doe not see how wee can thrive until we gett into a stock of slaves sufficient to doe all our business, for our children's children will hardly see this great Continent filled with people." The need for laborers was more pressing in the South where colonists had discovered that large-scale plantings of tobacco and rice were profitable. In 1661 the Virginia assembly found the answer to their labor problem. Negroes, the assembly ruled, were to be "perpetual servants." As other colonies followed Virginia's example, thousands of Africans were brought to North America. When a federal census was taken in 1790, Negroes were one fifth of the population.

The African in British America was a man without a country. Everything in this strange new land was different from what he had known at home. The long voyage on the slave ship and the months of "seasoning" were a kind of brainwashing that destroyed the past but gave him nothing to take its place.

In the West Indies and South America he was able to hold onto many of his African ways. Along the Atlantic seaboard there were no dense jungles and few mountain fastnesses where he could hole up with his fellows and build permanent settlements. This doesn't mean that the slaves didn't rebel or run away. They did. Virginia's Great Dismal Swamp and Okefenokee in Georgia offered shelter to runaways for more than a hundred years. So many made their way to Spanish Florida that the army had to mount a full-scale expedition to recapture them.

Year after year colonists heard reports of "an intended insurrection of the Negroes, which was to have been put in execution on Easter Day" . . . "a very wicked and barbarous plott of the Negroes" . . . "a Conspiracy to rise and forcibly make their Way out of the Province . . ." Usually these plots were "happily discovered" and the ringleaders executed. "Some were burnt, others hanged, one broke on the wheele, and one hung alive in chains," the governor of New York wrote after a rebellion there.

While the black man dreamed of freedom, his memories of Africa grew dim. At night in his lonely cabin he might tap out the rhythm of a song or recall a story that his father's father had told him. But he had no Ibo Club or Mandingo Society where he could go on Sundays to talk about the old country. On the slave ship he had been deliberately separated from his fellow villagers so that he rarely knew anyone who spoke his native tongue. His Great Gods hadn't followed him across the ocean and his knowledge of weaving or wood carving wasn't wanted in the New World.

So the African learned the white man's language and joined the white man's church. And on a warm afternoon in July 1776, he stood in the courtyard of the State House in Philadelphia and listened to the Declaration of Independence.

"—We hold these truths to be self-evident, that all men are created equal, that they are endowed by their Creator with certain inalienable Rights, that among these are Life, Liberty and the pursuit of Happiness."

"OH, HAIL COLUMBIA! HAPPY LAND!
  THE CRADLE LAND OF LIBERTY!
WHERE NONE BUT NEGROES BEAR THE BRAND,
  OR FEEL THE LASH OF SLAVERY.

THEN LET THE GLORIOUS ANTHEM PEAL!
  AND DROWN, 'BRITTANIA RULES THE WAVES'—
STRIKE UP THE SONG THAT MEN CAN FEEL—
  'COLUMBIA RULES THREE MILLION SLAVES!'"

The American Anti-Slavery Almanac, 1843

CHAPTER 4

The Rights of Man

To Form a More Perfect Union

Negro minutemen took part in the battles of Concord and Lexington. They fought at Bunker Hill. They crossed the Delaware with General Washington and shivered and starved at Valley Forge. More that five thousand black men served in the Continental army and navy, fighting and dying alongside their white countrymen.

All during the Revolution, they called for an end to slavery. "Although our Skins are different in Colour from those whom we serve, we perceive by our own Reflections that we are endowed with the same Faculties as our masters," a group of slaves in Connecticut said. "There is nothing that leads us to a belief that we are any more obliged to serve them, than they us. The more we consider of this matter, the more we are Convinced of our Right to be free."

"A Great Number of Blackes" signed a petition asking the

Massachusetts legislature for their freedom. "Every principle from which America has acted in the Course of their unhappy Dificulties with Great Briton Pleads Stronger than a thousand arguments in favor of your petitioners," they wrote.

The lawmakers agreed. They drew up a bill "preventing the practise of holding persons in Slavery" but it failed to pass when John Adams, Massachusetts' delegate to the Continental Congress warned that it might anger the South. "The bill for freeing the Negroes, I hope will sleep for a Time. We have Causes enough of Jealousy Discord and Division, and this Bill will certainly add to the Number," he wrote.

Then Quok Walker, a Massachusetts slave, tried a different path to freedom. He ran away from his master. Captured and beaten with a whip handle, he sued in the courts. Didn't the state constitution say that all men were born free? Wasn't he a man? The year the Revolution ended, the Massachusetts Supreme Court said "yes."

Quok Walker was free and slavery was dead in Massachusetts. It died a lingering death in the other states of the North during the next years, but it was given a new lease on life in the South.

By the end of the Revolution almost every patriot leader—Patrick Henry and Tom Paine, John Adams and Sam Adams, Alexander Hamilton and John Jay—was opposed to slavery. Washington hoped "to see some plan adopted by which slavery may be abolished." Jefferson wrote, "This abomination must have an end," and Franklin, president of the nation's first antislavery society, proposed that the slave trade be immediately outlawed.

Yet when delegates of the thirteen states met at the Constitutional Convention in 1787, no one spoke for the slave. The rights of man and the wrongs of slavery were not at issue. The problem was to form a strong federal government and the word of the day was "compromise."

The slave trade? The Constitution permitted it to continue for another twenty years.

Runaway slaves? Free states were ordered to return them to their masters.

Representation in Congress? The number of congressmen that a state sent to Washington was to be based on the size of its population. But were slaves a part of the population? After some debate, the delegates decided to count each slave as three fifths of a man. This meant that a planter who owned ten slaves had, in effect, seven votes while a citizen of a free state had one. This meant that the voteless black men gave power to southern whites that was far out of proportion to the number of whites.

"In order to form a more perfect Union, establish justice, insure domestic tranquility," as the preamble to the Constitution said, the world's first modern democracy recognized the right of one man to own another.

When the delegates returned to their homes, Jupiter Hammon, a soft-spoken slave poet, expressed his disappointment. "That liberty is a great thing we know from our own feelings, and we may likewise judge so from the conduct of the white people in the late war," he wrote in "An Address to Negroes in the State of New York." "I must say that I have hoped that God would open their eyes, when they were so much engaged for liberty, to think of the state of the poor blacks and to pity us."

Slavery's Chains

For another seventy-five years, slaves harvested tobacco in Virginia, picked cotton in South Carolina, planted sugar cane in Louisiana. They chopped down the tall Georgia pines, turned over the rich black soil of Mississippi and set out groves of orange trees in Florida.

J. M. WILSON

HAVING REMOVED TO THE

CORNER OF ESPLANADE & MOREAU STS.

NEW ORLEANS,

Will keep on hand and be constantly receiving during the season.

LARGE SUPPLIES OF

AND

VIRGINA NEGROES;

CONSISTING OF

Field Hands, House Servants, Cooks, Seamstresses, Washers and Ironers, Mechanics, &c,

ALL OF WHICH WILL BE SOLD

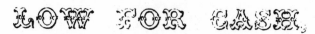

OR, ON TIME, FOR GOOD CITY ACCEPTANCE.

PLANTERS AND PURCHASERS

Generally are respectfully invited to

Call and Examine before Purchasing elsewhere.

Slave ironworkers tended forges and furnaces in Tennessee. Slaves mined coal in Virginia, iron in Kentucky, lead in Missouri. They built ships in the yards of Charleston and Baltimore, dug canals in North Carolina, put up bridges in Mississippi and laid more than a thousand miles of railroad in Georgia.

Slaves were shoemakers and barbers, ladies' maids and tailors. Slave blacksmiths constructed the delicate wrought-iron balconies of Natchez and New Orleans. Slave carpenters and bricklayers built the pillared plantation houses and slave gardeners planted their formal gardens. Slaves cooked and baked and served with a style that made "southern hospitality" known around the world.

For all this and more, the slave received not one cent in wages. He was given a peck of corn meal and three pounds of salt pork each week, a pair of shoes each year. His windowless cabin had a mud floor, a smoky chimney and a roof that leaked when it rained. He was often cold, always ragged, seldom healthy. Only three slaves out of a hundred lived beyond sixty. The average age of death for a slave was twenty-one.

If it was not the worst slavery in the world, it was one of the most degrading. The African who was brought to Latin America worked hard and died young too. But he was still considered a person with rights that his owner had to respect. He could testify in court if his master was cruel. He married in church and his wife and children could not be sold away from him. Most important of all, his slavery was not perpetual. If he earned money in his spare time, he could sign a contract with his owner which allowed him to buy his freedom. Once free, he was the equal of any other citizen in the land. In Brazil, Mexico, Puerto Rico, former slaves married Spanish and Portuguese colonists and took part in public life, according to their abilities.

In the United States a slave complained, "I can't go to anyone to be righted." In court his word had the same value as "the cry of an animal." "He can do nothing, possess nothing,

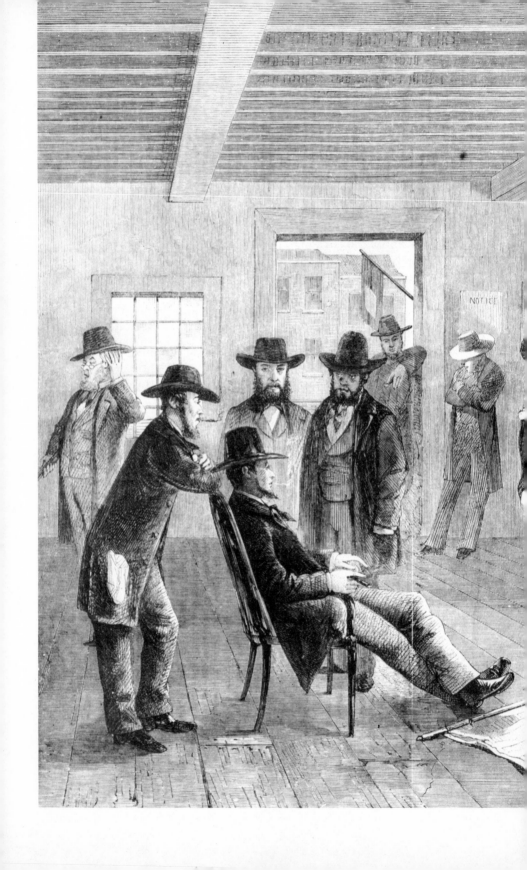

nor acquire anything but what must belong to his master," a Louisiana law declared. "The power of the master must be absolute, the submission of the slave perfect."

The South became a police state with laws that controlled every movement of the slaves. "If more than seven slaves together are found in any road without a white person, twenty lashes apiece; for visiting a plantation without a written pass, ten lashes; for hunting with dogs in the woods, thirty lashes; for riding in the night, or riding horses in the daytime without leave, a slave may be whipped, cropped or branded in the

Slave punishment

cheek with the letter R." Armed men on horseback patrolled the roads and special "Negro dogs" were trained to track down runaways.

But to get "perfect submission" took more than this. A slave had to be made to *feel* inferior to a white man. Schools for Negroes were forbidden. "Any person that teaches any person of color, slave or free, to read or write, is subjected to a fine of thirty dollars for each offense." In many cities it was a crime for a slave to own a book.

"Does a slave look dissatisfied? Does he speak loudly when spoken to by the master?" said an ex-slave, describing the thinking of a slaveholder. "Then he is getting high-minded, and should be taken down a button hole lower. Does he forget to pull off his hat at the approach of a white person? Then he is wanting in reverence. Does he venture to vindicate his conduct when censured? Then he is guilty of impudence, one of the greatest crimes of which a slave can be guilty."

Slave marriages had no standing. "The relation between slaves is essentially different from that of man and wife joined in lawful wedlock. With slaves it may be dissolved by the sale of one or both, depending on the caprice or necessity of the owners," a southern court ruled.

Slave children did not belong to their parents. "Boys weighing about 50 lbs. can be sold for about five hundred dollars," a South Carolina newspaper reported. "We were all put up at auction and sold to the highest bidder, and scattered over various parts of the country," a runaway slave said. "My brothers and sisters were bid off one by one, while my mother, holding my hand, looked on in an agony of grief."

Some men broke under the system and went quietly or noisily mad. Some women drowned their babies rather than see them grow up in slavery. Others endured. They lived from day to day, finding joy in simple pleasures—a 'possum treed after the week's work was done, a ham stolen from the master's smokehouse. And they took comfort from a religion that promised them a better life in the hereafter.

Runaway slave resists capture

The wonder is not that so many submitted, but that so many tried to throw off their chains. Some fought for their liberty with homemade daggers and pike heads. In 1800, Gabriel Prosser and a thousand slaves marched on the city of Richmond. In 1822, Denmark Vesey plotted a rebellion in Charleston in which upwards of nine thousand slaves were involved. In 1831, Nat Turner led an avenging army through Virginia, killing masters and their families.

These and other uprisings, large and small, were doomed to fail. The slaves with their homemade weapons were no match for the federal cavalry or the state militia. After each rebellion, the leaders were hanged and the slave laws made tighter. "The only principle that can maintain slavery," citizens of South Carolina decided when Vesey's plot was discovered, is "the principle of fear."

The Railroad

With all the odds against them, slaves ran away. Some hid in the swamps for a week or two and then gave themselves up. Others traveled a thousand miles to freedom. Charles Ball made his way on foot from Georgia to his wife's cabin in Maryland. William Hall paddled a canoe from Tennessee to the free state of Illinois. Henry Brown had himself nailed in a packing box and shipped by express from Richmond to Philadelphia. Frederick Douglass rode a train from Baltimore to New York with forged free papers in his pocket. Josiah Henson fled from Kentucky to Canada. Harriet Tubman walked from Maryland to Pennsylvania.

At the beginning of the nineteenth century they made their way alone. Later they traveled on the Underground Railroad. The Underground Railroad wasn't a real railroad. It was the

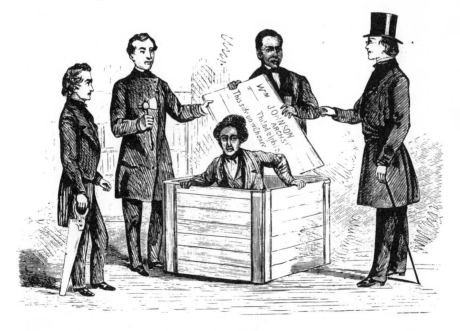

Henry "Box" Brown

first great movement of people who believed that slavery was wrong.

It was against the law for a slave to run away. It was against the law to hide him from the slave catchers who pursued him. But didn't the Bible say, "Thou shalt not deliver unto his master the servant which is escaped?" All over the United States freedom-loving Americans broke laws as a protest against slavery.

The lawbreakers' homes were the "stations" on the Underground Railroad, their wagons and buggies its "trains." The "tracks" ran across the Ohio River to the free states of the Midwest, across the Pennsylvania border to the free states of the Northeast and then on to Canada. Its "passengers" were the runaways who were hidden in attics, barns and secret rooms.

Negro and white worked together on the Underground Railroad. Most of the "conductors" were former slaves. Harriet Tubman and Josiah Henson risked their lives time and again to return to the South and lead family and friends to freedom. So did Laura Haviland, a middle-aged Quaker teacher, and John Fairfield who came from an aristocratic slaveholding family in Virginia. After twelve years of hair-raising adventures as a conductor, Fairfield was killed by slave catchers.

The "station masters" too were ordinary people with extraordinary courage. Storekeepers, farmers, peddlers, they fed and clothed the runaways before shipping them to the next station along the line. In the Midwest, Levi Coffin, a Quaker merchant, was called "President of the Underground Railroad" because he helped more than three thousand slaves to escape. In the East, the same title was given to Robert Purvis, a Negro farmer, whose home outside of Philadelphia sheltered nine thousand slaves in the years before the Civil War.

The records of the Underground Railroad were secret, so that the exact number of passengers it carried is not known. However, a Mississippi governor estimated that one hundred thousand slaves escaped from the South between 1810 and 1850.

Harriet Tubman

CHAPTER 5

At the North

Halfway to Heaven

"I looked at my hands to see if I was the same person," Harriet Tubman said of the time when she first entered a free state. "There was such a glory over everything. The sun came like gold through the trees and I felt like I was in heaven."

In the early years of the Republic, Negroes in the North shared Harriet's feelings. Paul Cuffe, son of an American freedman and an Indian girl, built up a fleet of merchant ships that regularly crossed the Atlantic. Benjamin Banneker, grandson of an African chief and an English servingmaid, was a member of the team of surveyors who laid out the city of Washington, D.C. James Forten, a veteran of the Revolution, became the owner of a sail loft where U. S. Navy vessels were outfitted.

Hadn't de Crèvecoeur said, "If thou wilt work, thou shalt prosper"? They too believed in the American dream of freedom and equality for all. But as the eighteenth century gave way to the nineteenth, their hopes were drowned in a rising tide of prejudice.

The word "prejudice" comes from "prejudge," meaning to pass judgment or pronounce sentence before trial. Negro Americans were judged by a simple association of ideas:

Black men came to America as slaves. Slaves are inferior. Therefore black men are inferior.

The conclusion was illogical, nonsensical—and tragically difficult to disprove. Negroes had no body of scientific evidence on their side. Biologists had not yet discovered the origins of man. There were no historians or anthropologists with a knowledge of African civilizations.

White Americans knew only what they saw. A Negro *looked* different. Because of his dark skin, he was judged inferior and sentenced to live apart. The sentence was for life, with no time off for good behavior.

Public schools opened—and Negro children were not allowed to attend them. "They are not by nature equal to the whites and their children cannot be made equal to my children," an Iowan declared. Separate schools for Negroes were established, but they were never as good as the white schools. Rhode Island Negroes complained that their children's teachers were "indifferent" and underpaid. In Connecticut, school officials found

Negro children turned away from school

Negro schools "excessively crowded and destitute of some of the first requisites." Educators in New York contrasted the "splendid almost palatial edifices" for white children with the "old and dilapidated buildings" for blacks. In San Francisco, the colored school was in a badly ventilated basement. "The plastering is broken and falling from the ceiling, so that the water from above runs through the floor upon the desks of the schoolroom beneath," Negro parents said.

Even private schools ran into trouble if they accepted Negro pupils. In 1835, Noyes Academy in Canaan, New Hampshire, admitted fourteen Negro students "to afford colored youth a fair opportunity, equally with whites, of improving themselves," the trustees explained. The boys remained in the Academy for five months, until the citizens of Canaan voted at a town meeting to get rid of them. They did this quickly and efficiently by hitching one hundred yoke of oxen to the foundations of the school and towing it away.

"Fourteen black boys with books in their hands set the entire Granite State crazy!" said Alexander Crummell, one of the black boys in question.

"Why should I strive hard and acquire all the constituents of a man if the prevailing genius of the land admit me not as such?" another black boy asked. He was the top student in New York's African Free School but he wondered, "What are my prospects? Shall I be a mechanic? No one will employ me. Drudgery and servitude, then, are my prospective portion. Can you be surprised at my discouragement?"

Wherever the boy looked, he saw roadblocks. His father might have been a slave blacksmith, carpenter, tailor. But most trades were closed to free Negroes by the beginning of the nineteenth century. The boy could go to sea on a whaler or a clipper ship headed for China. If he remained on land the best he could hope for was work as a waiter, porter, day laborer, while his sister scrubbed clothes or cooked for a livelihood.

He could take his best girl for a walk in the park on Saturday night, but he could not ride with her in a horsecar unless it was labeled COLORED. Museums and zoos turned him away. Theater owners sent him to the gallery, churches to a special "Negro pew." He could not buy refreshments in an ice cream parlor or an oyster bar. When "The Black Swan," a Negro contralto, sang in Metropolitan Hall, advertisements for her concert carried a "Particular Notice: No colored person can be admitted, as there is no part of the house appropriated for them."

The Negro's prospects grew worse after the first wave of immigrants arrived. "These impoverished and destitute beings are crowding themselves into every place of business and driving the poor colored American citizen out," Negro newspapers complained. "Every hour sees us elbowed out of some employment to make room for newly arrived immigrants whose hunger and color are thought to give them a title to especial favor."

Before long, Irishmen outnumbered Negroes in the eastern cities. As the two groups competed for the same menial jobs, the newcomers quickly learned American ways. The Negroes were the Got-Here-Firsts, but the Irish, after all, were white. No matter how ragged and miserable they were they could always comfort themselves by shouting, "Down with the blacks! Let them go back to Africa where they belong."

The "Back to Africa" slogan was not invented by the Irish, however. It started with a group of businessmen, Northerners and Southerners, who thought that free black men were a threat to the slave system. Forming the American Colonization Society, they bought land in Africa as a "homeland" for free Negroes from the United States. Liberia, the colony they established, failed to attract many settlers, but the Colonization Society's insistence on the United States as "a white man's country" helped transform race prejudice into race hatred.

During periods of unemployment "Back to Africa" became a rallying cry for jobless whites who stormed through Negro neighborhoods with clubs and torches. Time and again there were riots in northern cities in which black men were beaten and their homes burned. In 1829 a white mob forced more than half the Negroes of Cincinnati to flee to Canada. A similar riot in Philadelphia five years later drove hundreds of families from the city. The citizens committee investigating the riot blamed it on the fact that Negroes had jobs while whites were unemployed. They advised Negroes to behave "inoffensively at all times; taking care, as they pass along the street, or assemble together, not to be obtrusive."

Why didn't the young New Yorker or Philadelphian seek his fortune in the West? Sometimes he did. But the state of Ohio required that a Negro settler post a $500 bond guaranteeing good conduct. Illinois demanded a $1000 bond and Indiana flatly said, "We want none of you here." The public lands in the western territories were open to homesteaders from Europe, but they were closed to Americans with dark skins.

Before the revolution, free men of color voted even in the southern colonies. Afterward, they lost this right almost everywhere. A black New Yorker whose family had lived in the state for two centuries could not vote unless he owned $250 worth of real estate, but a penniless immigrant was welcomed at the polls. New Jersey, Connecticut and Pennsylvania banned Negro voters no matter how much property they owned. And in Oregon, a Negro was not even allowed to own property.

A black man could not testify against a white in the courts of California, Illinois, Indiana, Iowa, Ohio. He could not serve on a jury except in Massachusetts. It was seldom possible for him to win a law suit or have a fair trial.

As far as the federal government was concerned, Negroes were forbidden to join the militia or enlist in the Marine Corps. They were accepted in the Navy only as cooks or stewards. The Secretary of State refused them passports when they traveled abroad and the Postmaster General objected to their presence in the post office. In a confidential letter to Congress he explained that Negro postmen might learn "that a man's rights do not depend on his color." Taking note of the warning, Congress ruled that "no other than a free white person shall be employed in conveying the mail."

Bad as this was, there was worse to come. In 1857 the Supreme Court heard the case of Dred Scott, a slave who claimed his freedom because his master had taken him to a free state. "The question is simply this," Chief Justice Roger Taney explained. "Can a Negro whose ancestors were sold as slaves become a member of the political community brought into existence by the Constitution, and as such become entitled to all the rights and privileges guaranteed to the citizens?"

No, the Court decided. Negroes "were not intended to be included under the word 'citizens' in the Constitution and can therefore claim none of the rights and privileges which that instrument provides."

Since the Revolution Negro Americans had been second-class citizens. Now the Supreme Court had found that they were not citizens at all.

Freedom Fighters

All during these years, Negroes campaigned for equal rights. As early as 1780, Paul Cuffe and six other Massachusetts men petitioned the legislature because they paid taxes but were not allowed to vote. Benjamin Banneker sent Thomas Jefferson a copy of an almanac he had written, to show that "the African race" was "capable of mental endowments." He appealed to the author of the Declaration of Independence to "embrace every opportunity to eradicate that train of absurd and false ideas which so generally prevails with respect to us."

"Has the God who made the white man and the black left any record declaring us a different species?" James Forten asked. "Are we not supported by the same food, hurt by the same wounds, pleased with the same delights? And should we not then enjoy the same liberty and be protected by the same laws?"

Born in 1776, Forten served in the Revolutionary navy as a

powder boy. Afterward he was apprenticed to a sailmaker. When he invented a new way of handling sails he went into business for himself. Wealthy and respected, he made his spacious home in Philadelphia a headquarters in the fight against discrimination. In 1813, his *Series of Letters by a Man of Color* helped defeat a bill that would have prevented free Negroes from entering Pennsylvania. He was less successful some years later when the state constitution was revised and black men were denied the ballot. The year that the new constitution went into effect, Philadelphians watched a strange procession on Election Day. Stately James Forten, wearing the black broadcloth of a gentleman, led a group of white workingmen to the polls. He was bringing his employees to vote as a way of protesting his own loss of rights.

When the American Colonization Society was started, its leaders called on Forten for support. A merchant of his standing, they slyly pointed out, could easily become the ruler of Liberia.

"I would rather remain as James Forten, sailmaker, in Philadelphia than enjoy the highest office in the gift of your society," he retorted.

At meeting after meeting, he urged Negroes to reject the plan "to exile us from the land of our nativity." "My great-grandfather was brought to this country as a slave," he told a white gathering. "My grandfather obtained his own freedom. My father rendered valuable service to his country in the war of our Revolution. I have labored in a useful employment, have gathered property and have paid taxes in this city. Yet some ingenious gentlemen have recently discovered that a continent three thousand miles from the place where I was born is my native country. And I am advised to go home."

Active in Negro churches and educational societies, Forten was also an organizer of the first national Negro convention. Following the Cincinnati riot of 1829, men from eight eastern states traveled to Philadelphia to establish the American Society of Free Persons of Colour. Alarmed by the expulsion of Negroes from Ohio, the delegates recommended not Africa but Canada as a refuge.

While Negro conventions continued to meet and to protest against "cruel and oppressive laws," Negroes also joined forces with white antislavery men. After the American Anti-Slavery Society was formed in 1833, both Forten and his son-in-law Robert Purvis served on its board of managers. The society called for the immediate abolition of slavery and an end to prejudice against colored people. It proposed to bring this about by appealing to the conscience of the nation.

The next years saw an outpouring of antislavery books, pamphlets, newspapers, all aimed at convincing "our fellow citizens that slaveholding is a heinous crime in the sight of God." The South quickly reacted by suppressing antislavery publications, mobbing antislavery speakers and declaring that "slavery is a positive good." But the abolitionists made headway in the North. Women formed female antislavery societies and sewed clothing for runaway slaves. Children joined junior societies and sang antislavery songs at bazaars and picnics held to raise money for the movement. By the time James Forten died in 1842, there were two thousand state and local antislavery groups with upwards of two hundred thousand members.

As a way of demonstrating to white audiences that a Negro was "a man and a brother," black men and women spoke at the antislavery meetings. Some were Northerners who had managed to break through the wall of color to become college graduates, editors, doctors. Others were ex-slaves who could speak at firsthand of the horrors of slavery—people like William Wells Brown, Josiah Henson, Harriet Tubman and Frederick Douglass.

Born in 1817, Douglass was twenty when he escaped from his master. Four years later he became a lecturer for the Massachusetts Anti-Slavery Society. An editor who heard one of his first speeches came away dazzled. "This is an extraordinary man. He was cut out for a hero," he wrote. "A commanding

THE
AMERICAN
ANTI-SLAVERY
ALMANAC,

FOR

1840,

BEING BISSEXTILE OR LEAP-YEAR, AND THE 64TH OF AMERICAN
INDEPENDENCE.   CALCULATED FOR BOSTON ; ADAPTED:
TO THE NEW ENGLAND STATES.

NORTHERN HOSPITALITY—NEW YORK NINE MONTHS' LAW.
The slave steps out of the slave-state, and his chains fall.   A free state, with another
chain, stands ready to re-enslave him. ·

Thus saith the Lord, Deliver him that is spoiled out of the hands of the oppressor.

NEW YORK & BOSTON :
PUBLISHED BY THE AMERICAN ANTI-SLAVERY SOCIETY,
NO. 143 NASSAU STREET, NEW YORK ; ·
AND BY J. A. COLLINS, 29 CORNHILL, BOSTON.

person over six feet in height and of most manly proportions. As a speaker he has wit, arguments, sarcasm, pathos. His voice is highly melodious and rich and his enunciation quite elegant."

Frederick Douglass remained the Negro's leading spokesman for more than fifty years. Although he had never had a day of schooling, he was soon an accomplished writer as well as orator. His *Narrative of the Life of Frederick Douglass* became a best seller and in 1847 he started his own newspaper, *The North Star.*

Although many of his white associates advised him against the venture, he explained in his first issue: "The man who has

Frederick Douglass

'suffered the wrong is the man to demand redress—the man STRUCK is the man to CRY OUT—he who has endured the cruel pangs of Slavery is the man to advocate Liberty. We must be our own representatives and advocates—not distinct from, but in connection with our white friends."

While commenting on every issue of the day from votes for women to the Mexican War, many of Douglass' blistering editorials were devoted to "colorphobia"—the "strange plague" that afflicted white men whenever their darker brethren entered a restaurant or railroad train. He described the symptoms: "a red and furious look about the cheek, the hand clinched, head shaking, teeth grating. Pointing with outstretched arm towards us, its victims would exclaim, 'Look! look!' 'Don't you see?' 'See what?' 'Why, that BLACK!' Then, with eyes turned up in horror, they would start off in a furious gallop, running all around us, and gazing at us, as if they would read our very hearts. The whole scene was deeply afflicting and terrible."

As a cure for the epidemic, Douglass recommended resistance. He walked out of a church that assigned him a separate seat. He refused to leave a restaurant without being served or to move from the first-class car on a train. More than once he was beaten for his refusal and forcibly thrown out.

By the middle of the nineteenth century Negroes were joining together to fight discrimination. In Massachusetts they boycotted the railroads until the special "colored cars" were abolished. They were less successful in New York where the right to ride on a horsecar depended on the conductor's mood.

One Sunday morning in 1854, Elizabeth Jennings, a Negro school teacher, tried to board a Third Avenue car. The conductor blocked her way.

"You'll have to wait. Next car's reserved for your people," he said.

"I have no people," Miss Jennings answered. "I wish to go to church and I don't wish to be detained."

When the conductor threatened her, she grew stubborn. "I

am a respectable person, born and brought up in New York and I was never so insulted before," she said.

"I was born in Ireland," the conductor retorted, "and you've got to get out of this car."

He pushed. She clung to the window. The driver came to the conductor's assistance and together they tossed her into the gutter. To their surprise, she climbed back into the car again. This time the driver galloped his horses down the street until he found a policeman. The three men finally succeeded in pushing Elizabeth Jennings from the car.

Badly bruised, she made her way home on foot. But she had written down the number of the car. The next day she told her story to the Legal Rights Association, a newly formed Negro organization. With the help of their lawyer, Chester A. Arthur, later President of the United States, they took Elizabeth Jennings' case to court—and won it. She was awarded damages of $225 and conductors were ordered to admit all respectable people, white and colored, to the horsecars.

The victory was a limited one. The following year a New York jury decided against a Negro minister who was forced out of a railroad train. And streetcars remained segregated in Philadelphia, Washington, Cincinnati and other major cities until the end of the Civil War.

More than anything else, Negro parents wanted good schools for their children. "The point which we must aim at," Frederick Douglass said, "is to obtain admission for our children into the nearest and the best school house in our respective neighborhoods." In Boston, Negroes protested regularly against separate colored schools—and were just as regularly turned down. In one report, the School Committee noted that the Pilgrim fathers had not objected to being separated from the Indians. Why then should Negroes object to *their* separation?

The parents were not satisfied with this reasoning. Every morning Sarah Roberts walked past five white primary schools in order to reach the Smith Street School for Colored Children. In 1849 her father filed suit against the city of Boston. Carrying the case to the state supreme court, his lawyer, Charles Sumner, argued that a separate school could never be equal to one that was integrated. "The matters taught in the two schools may be precisely the same," he said, "but a school devoted to one class must differ essentially in spirit and character from that Common School where all classes meet together in Equality."

The court decided against Sarah Roberts, finding that the School Committee had done its duty by providing her with a school that was "separate but equal." It was a decision that would haunt Negro Americans for more than a century.

Meanwhile, Negroes in Boston formed an Equal School Rights Committee and deluged the legislature with petitions for integrated schools. Taking their children out of the Smith Street School, they had them taught privately until the legislature gave in. On a Monday morning in September 1855, the city's colored children went to the schools nearest their homes.

"Good-by forever," a boy shouted as he passed the shuttered windows of the school on Smith Street. "Now we are like other Boston boys!"

Massachusetts was far ahead of the rest of the nation. In Philadelphia, Charlotte Forten, James Forten's granddaughter, was tutored at home because her father refused to send her to the ramshackle school for colored. When she was sixteen, she boarded with friends in Salem, Massachusetts, so that she could go to a school which was open to everyone. After her graduation, she was hired as a teacher in Salem, becoming one of the first Negroes in the country to teach white girls and boys.

In Rochester, New York, Frederick Douglass wrote that "in no emergency will we send a child of ours to the miserable cellar" where the city's Negro children were taught. Instead he entered his nine-year-old daughter, Rosetta, in Seward Seminary, a private girls' school. Away lecturing when the school term started, he returned to find Rosetta in tears.

"I get along pretty well in school," she explained, "but the principal doesn't allow me into the room with the other scholars because I'm colored."

Forced to sit in a separate room with a teacher who came in occasionally to go over her lessons, Rosetta was not even permitted in the yard at recess when the other girls played games.

After Douglass stormed into the principal's office, she agreed to change her policy if all of Rosetta's schoolmates voted to accept her. Polled one by one, every girl in Seward Seminary agreed to have Rosetta in their classroom. But one parent objected and she was sent home.

In a stinging public letter to "the only person who was hardened and mean enough to degrade an innocent child" Douglass called on the liberal people of Rochester "to see that justice is done." While Rosetta went off to boarding school and then to Oberlin College in Ohio, he kept up his appeals. Rosetta was eighteen when her father finally succeeded in closing Rochester's colored schools. However, the law that permitted colored schools in other New York State towns remained in force until 1900.

"BRETHREN, ARISE, ARISE! STRIKE FOR
YOUR LIVES AND LIBERTIES.
NOW IS THE DAY AND THE HOUR.
LET EVERY SLAVE THROUGHOUT THE LAND DO THIS,
AND THE DAYS OF SLAVERY ARE NUMBERED.
Rather die freemen than live to be slaves.
REMEMBER THAT YOU ARE FOUR MILLIONS!"

*Rev. Henry Highland Garnet in An Address
to the Slaves of the United States, 1843*

CHAPTER 6

The Gathering Storm

Somebody Must Die

In the early days of the antislavery movement, most of its
leaders believed in nonviolence. They thought that they could
win freedom for the slaves by a revolution in public opinion,
rather than with swords and guns. There were always a few
men who disagreed. In 1828 the nation was startled by David
Walker's "Appeal to the Colored Citizens of the World" in
which he called on slaves to rebel and "kill or be killed."

Walker was a free Negro who had traveled through the
South before settling in Boston. He started off his eighty-eight
page "Appeal" in scholarly fashion by comparing the slaves of
ancient times to those in the United States. "We, the Blacks,
are treated more cruel by the white Christians of America,
than devils themselves ever treated a set of men, women and
children on this earth," he declared.

"Remember, Americans," he warned. "We must and shall be
free. You may do your best to keep us in wretchedness and
misery, to enrich you and your children, but God will deliver

us. And wo, wo, will be to you if we have to obtain our freedom by fighting. Throw away your fears and prejudices then, and treat us like men, and we will like you more than we do now hate you." "You are not astonished at my saying we hate you," he added in a footnote, "for if we are men, we cannot but hate you, while you are treating us like dogs."

Walker's "Appeal" was a remarkable piece of writing for a self-taught man who owned a clothing store. He printed it himself and with the help of Negro sailors smuggled hundreds of copies into the slave states. As the "Appeal" found its way into black hands, a wave of panic swept across the South. Ships were searched and Negro crewmen were not allowed to land. State after state put new teeth in the laws forbidding slaves to read and made it a crime, punishable by death, for a Negro to distribute antislavery writings.

The mayor of Savannah and the governor of Georgia wrote to Boston's Mayor Otis, begging him to stop Walker's "highly inflammatory" work. After sending a man around to the clothing store, Otis replied that since Walker was not violating a Massachusetts law, there was no way to stop him.

No way? Reports soon circulated in Boston that a group of Georgia men was offering a $3000 reward to anyone who would take David Walker's life. His friends advised him to go to Canada, but he refused to run away.

"I'll stand my ground," he said. "Somebody must die in this cause."

A year later, David Walker was dead. Whether he died of poison or from natural causes is still a mystery. The "Appeal" lived on. Too radical for most abolitionists when it was first published, it was reprinted and read with interest twenty years later. By then, antislavery men were losing faith in a peaceful revolution.

"We have seen the number of slaves increase from half a million to four millions," Frederick Douglass wrote. "The ten thousand enormities daily occurring in the Southern states have been flung before the public by ten thousand eloquent lips and by more than ten thousand eloquent pens. Instead of the slave holder becoming more disposed to listen to the suggestions of reason, his grip has become tighter, his conscience more and more callous."

Disobey This Law!

Each year the South demanded more territory and gained more power in the federal government. After Congress passed the Fugitive Slave Act of 1850, firm believers in nonviolence went out and bought guns.

Under the new law, a slave catcher had only to bring a colored man before a federal commissioner and swear that he was a runaway. Without giving the Negro a chance to be heard, the commissioner could then order his return to his owner. Since the slave catcher's word was all the proof that was required, any black man in the North could be "identified" as a slave and carried away.

Thousands of despairing Negroes packed their belongings and moved to Canada. Others talked of migrating to Africa, Haiti, Central America—and still others formed vigilance committees and prepared to defend their liberty with their lives. "Every colored man in the country should sleep with his revolver under his head, loaded and ready for use," Frederick Douglass advised.

Many did.

William Parker, a Negro farmer, lived in a two-story stone house in Christiana, Pennsylvania. Close to the Maryland border, his home had long been a station on the Underground Railroad. On a September night in 1851 he received word from the Philadelphia Vigilance Committee that a party of slave owners was headed his way. When they arrived at dawn the next day, accompanied by a federal marshal, Parker was ready.

While he talked with them, Mrs. Parker blew a horn from an upstairs window. The horn was a signal for all the Negroes

The Christiana rebellion

in the neighborhood to come to the defense of the runaways. They came on the double—twenty, thirty, forty men, armed with ax handles, corn cutters, guns.

For an hour the two groups faced each other. The marshal had a warrant for the arrest of the fugitives, but their defenders refused to let it be served. As tension mounted Parker appeared in his doorway.

"You'd better go away, if you don't want to get hurt," he advised.

Angered by his defiance, a slave owner drew his pistol. He shot. The Negroes answered, and the battle was on. Before the morning was over, two white men were stretched out on the grass in William Parker's yard. One was dead, the other badly hurt. Although several of Parker's comrades had bullet holes through their clothing, none suffered more than flesh wounds.

Negroes with guns in their hands had killed a white man! It didn't matter if they had acted in self-defense. Reports of "the shocking affair at Christiana" were telegraphed across the country. "The resisting of a law of Congress by a band of armed Negroes is more than a mere ordinary riot," a Philadelphia newspaper declared. "It is an act of insurrection."

A day later, U.S. marines marched into Christiana. With a posse of special constables they combed the countryside, breaking into homes of colored people and arresting everyone they could find. They never captured Parker. Spirited away by Underground Railroad workers he was safe in Canada. But forty other men and women, including three whites who had refused to help the slave catchers, were jailed. The charge against them was treason—that they "did traitorously assemble to oppose the execution of the laws of the United States and with force and arms did levy war against the United States."

The charge was so preposterous and the Fugitive Slave Law so unpopular that public sympathy shifted to the side of the "traitors." Defended by Congressman Thaddeus Stevens and other prominent Pennsylvania lawyers, they were found not guilty.

"Slaveholders were taught the wholesome lesson that the Fugitive Slave Law was no guarantee against red hot shot," observed William Still, chairman of Philadelphia's vigilance committee. "The Deputy Marshal likewise considered the business of catching slaves very unsafe."

Three weeks after the stand in Christiana, a pealing church bell announced the capture of a fugitive in Syracuse, New York. Under cover of darkness, antislavery men battered down the courthouse door with a log and carried off Jerry McHenry. When a similar attempt at rescue failed in Boston, not only marines but a regiment of artillery and a U. S. Coast Guard vessel were needed to return Anthony Burns to the South.

In Mechanicsburg, Ohio, the "whole damn abolition town" turned out to save Addison White from slave catchers. Across the state in Wellington, Negroes and whites took John Price

John Brown at Harpers Ferry

from the hands of federal marshals and sent him on to Canada. In Milwaukee, more than five thousand men stormed a jail to free Joshua Glover.

And then there was John Brown. "Though a white gentleman," Frederick Douglass reported when they first met, he "is in sympathy a black man." Believing that "slavery was a state of war," Brown went further than David Walker. He made plans to invade the South with a small band of guerrilla fighters. From hide-outs in the Allegheny Mountains, his men would swoop down on the plantations and free the slaves.

On a moonless October night in 1859, John Brown put his plan into action. With twenty-one men, a third of them Negroes, he captured the U.S. arsenal at Harpers Ferry, West Virginia. This time the marines were called out in full force, and the charge of treason stood. John Brown and six of his men were hanged. But in the weeks before their execution slavery and not Brown went on trial before the world.

Men who had never before concerned themselves with the plight of the slaves found themselves shaken. Was John Brown an outlaw, a murderer, or was he, as Ralph Waldo Emerson said, "that new saint who will make the gallows as glorious as the cross"? If Brown was right, then slavery was wrong. And if slavery was wrong . . .

A year after John Brown's raid, Abraham Lincoln was elected President of the United States. A month after the election, South Carolina seceded from the Union.

The war that would end slavery had begun.

"ONCE LET THE BLACK MAN GET UPON HIS
PERSON THE BRASS LETTERS U.S.; LET HIM
GET AN EAGLE ON HIS BUTTON, AND A MUSKET
ON HIS SHOULDER, AND BULLETS IN HIS
POCKET, AND THERE IS NO POWER ON EARTH
WHICH CAN DENY THAT HE EARNED THE
RIGHT OF CITIZENSHIP IN THE UNITED STATES."

Frederick Douglass

CHAPTER 7

Years of Hope

The Black Yankees

Days after President Lincoln called for volunteers to put down
the rebellion, he was swamped with offers from colored men.
In New York a newspaper reported, "a number of Blacks
quietly hired a public hall and commenced drilling, in view of
the possibility of a call to active service." In Philadelphia,
"The blacks are drilling on their own hook. They could muster
5,000 easily." The Negroes of Cincinnati formed a company of
Home Guards. "Attucks Guards" were organized in Albany,
Ohio, "Hannibal Guards" in Pittsburgh.

"We are ready to stand by and defend the government with
our lives, our fortunes and our sacred honor," a Boston mass
meeting resolved. "Colored women would go as nurses, seam-
stresses and warriors, if need be."

A Detroit doctor offered to raise "from 5,000 to 10,000 freemen to take any position assigned us (sharpshooters preferred)."

"We as colored citizens of Cleveland, are ready to go forth
and do battle in the common cause of the country."

"I know of some 300 of reliable colored free citizens of this City, who desire to enter the service," a Washington Negro wrote.

To each offer the answer was the same. "This Department has no intention to call into the service any colored soldiers . . . Your patriotic letter is received, and in reply would say, the Constitution will not permit me to issue the order." New York's police chief closed the hall where Negroes were drilling. The police of Cincinnati were even blunter. "We want you d—d niggers to keep out," they warned the Home Guard. "This is a white man's war."

Northerners were sure that the fighting would be over in a month or at the most ninety days. Then everything would be as it was before. Hadn't Lincoln announced that he did not intend "to interfere with the institution of slavery"?

Ninety days passed, and then another ninety. The "white man's war" was going badly for the Union. And no wonder, said Frederick Douglass. "We are fighting the rebels with only one hand, when we ought to be fighting them with both. We are striking with our soft white hand, when we should be striking with the iron hand of the black man, which we keep chained behind us."

Not Douglass but the slaves themselves began to interfere with the institution of slavery. Wherever Union armies appeared in the South, black men and women ran off to join them. Some Union officers returned the slaves to their owners. Others, hard-pressed and shorthanded, put them to work building forts, driving wagons, digging ditches.

The war dragged on. The numbers of dead and wounded mounted. At the end of the second summer of fighting, Secretary of War Stanton sent a quiet order to a field commander in the South—arm the blacks. President Lincoln followed this with his proclamation of emancipation. On January 1, 1863: "All persons held as slaves" in the rebel states would be "thenceforward, and forever, free." "And I further declare," he wrote, "that such persons, of suitable condition, will be received into the armed service of the United States."

Negro soldiers

Negroes wept, cheered, prayed and joined the army. Slogging through the mud of Louisiana, South Carolina, Florida they sang:

So rally, boys, rally, let us never mind the past.
We had a hard road to travel, but our day is coming fast,
For God is for the right, and we have no need to fear—
The Union must be saved by the colored volunteer.

They charged up the ramparts of Port Hudson and Fort Wagner. They fought at Milliken's Bend and Vicksburg, Nashville, Mobile and Petersburg.

Under white officers, the colored troops were given more than their share of duty and less than their share of pay. In battle, they faced a double risk because the rebels, in violation of all the laws of war, either shot Negroes or sold them as slaves if they were captured. But they also won a double victory.

"You have no idea how my prejudices with regard to Negro troops have been dispelled by the battle the other day," an officer declared. "The brigade of Negroes behaved magnificently and fought splendidly. They are far superior in discipline to the white troops and just as brave."

At last the fighting drew to a close. On an April day in 1865, Jefferson Davis, president of the Confederacy, packed his belongings and fled from Richmond. Soon a cry echoed through the city: "The Yankees are coming!"

As Virginians watched from behind curtained windows, a troop of Negro cavalrymen galloped down the street. Reining in their horses, the black Yankees raised the United States flag above the capitol of the Confederacy.

Our Common Brotherhood

The war was won and the slaves were free. "Everything around us indicates a change in our condition," a Negro newspaperman said. The Attorney General had declared that the Dred Scott decision was wrong. Congress repealed the law banning Negroes from the post office. Frederick Douglass was a welcome visitor at the White House and Sojourner Truth, another ex-slave, won the right to ride in the streetcars of Washington.

"Were I a drinker I would get on a Jolly spree, but as a Christian I can but kneel in prayer and bless God," wrote a colored resident of the capital.

Negroes across the country organized a National Equal Rights League, with John Mercer Langston, an Ohio lawyer, as president. The League called on the nation "to destroy restrictions which prevent colored people from entering libraries, colleges, lecture rooms, military academies, jury boxes, churches, thea-

Negro·troops

tres, street cars and from voting . . . We ask of the people a patient hearing and admission to our common brotherhood, the human race."

For a time it seemed as if they would win their demands. The word on everyone's lips in the first year of peace was "reconstruction"—to rebuild, make over. The rebels were expected to remake their state governments before they could return to the Union. They would have to accept the abolition of slavery and, Lincoln had suggested, "adopt some system by which the two races could lift themselves out of their old relation to each other, and come out better prepared for the new."

But Lincoln was dead and the white men of the South had no intention of building a new relationship between the races. They still preferred the old one. In the first year of peace, each rebel state passed laws, known as black codes, which were designed to keep the Negro "in his place." "Servants" (black) were required to sign yearly contracts to work for "masters" (white). If a freedman quit his job before the year was out, he could be arrested and forced to labor on roads and levees without pay. Negroes were forbidden to carry guns or make alcoholic beverages. In Mississippi they could not buy or rent farm land. In South Carolina they were not allowed to go into business for themselves unless they bought special and expensive licenses. In some Louisiana towns they could not walk on the streets after dark without passes signed by their "masters."

Congressman Carl Schurz who toured the South at the request of President Andrew Johnson reported on the popular notion that "the Negro exists for the special object of raising cotton, rice and sugar for the whites, and that it is illegitimate for him to indulge, like other people, in the pursuit of his own happiness.

"The whites esteem the blacks their property by natural right. However much they admit that the individual relations of masters and slaves have been destroyed by the war, they still

HARPER'S WEEKLY.

A JOURNAL OF CIVILIZATION.

Vol. XI.—No. 568.]   NEW YORK, SATURDAY, NOVEMBER 16, 1867.   [SINGLE COPIES TEN CENTS. $4.00 PER YEAR IN ADVANCE.

Entered according to Act of Congress, in the Year 1867, by Harper & Brothers, in the Clerk's Office of the District Court for the Southern District of New York.

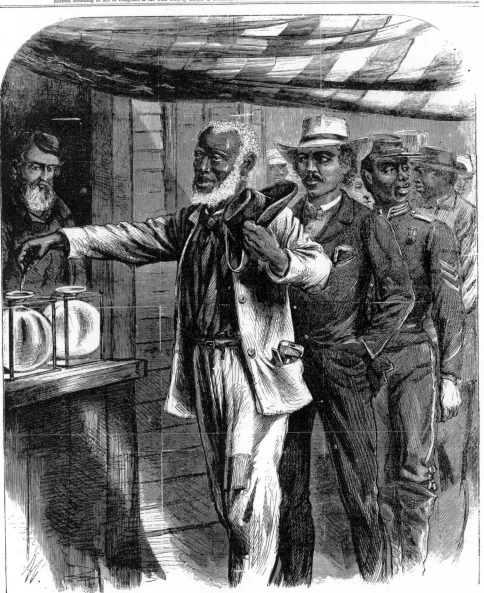

"The First Vote"

have an ingrained feeling that the blacks at large belong to the whites at large."

The South's attempt to turn back the clock to slavery days shocked the rest of the country. The courage of Negro soldiers had started a ground swell of good will in the North. Even men who still cherished their own prejudices wanted fair treatment for the freedmen.

"The men of the North will convert Mississippi into a frog pond," warned the Chicago *Tribune,* "before they will allow such laws to disgrace one foot of soil in which the bones of our soldiers sleep and over which the flag of freedom waves." "The South called for war," James Russell Lowell reminded his readers. "We will fix the terms of peace ourselves and teach the South that Christ is disguised in a dusky race." When the passage of the black codes was followed by bloody riots in Memphis and New Orleans in which hundreds of Negroes were killed and injured, Congress took over the job of reconstruction.

In 1866 the nation's first Civil Rights Act was passed. It was a bill that declared that all persons born in the United States (except Indians) were entitled to equal rights before the law. After this came the Fourteenth and Fifteenth Amendments to the Constitution. Black men were finally, legally, citizens of the United States with their right to vote guaranteed by the Constitution. The Negro owed his sweeping victory not to his friends alone, commented Congressman Julian of Ohio, but "to the desperate madness of his enemies."

All during the summer of 1867 black men in the South marched to open-air rallies, listened to stump speakers, joined political clubs. In the fall seven hundred thousand Negroes went to the polls. While regiments of soldiers stood guard, they voted to reconstruct their state governments and return to the Union. The following year, black men and white men met in the capital cities of the old Confederacy and wrote new state constitutions.

They dropped the old property qualifications that had kept thousands of poor whites from voting. They repealed the black

Congressman J. Willis Menard of Louisiana addressing the House of Representatives

codes and abolished imprisonment for debt. They opened the state universities to everyone, regardless of color, and they established systems of free public schools. For two hundred years the South had been ruled by rich planters. Now, for the first time, its people had a democratic government.

During the next eight years, Negroes sat in state legislatures and went to Washington as senators and congressmen. Black Oscar Dunn and near-white P. B. S. Pinchback served as lieutenant governors of Louisiana. Jonathan Gibbs was superintendent of public instruction in Florida. Francis L. Cardozo gave up schoolteaching to become South Carolina's secretary of state, while James Hill held the same office in Mississippi. From Virginia to Texas, there were Negro sheriffs and policemen, judges and jurors, postmasters and clerks. The professor of philosophy at the University of South Carolina was a black man. So was the mayor of Natchez.

On the floor of the House of Representatives, brown-skinned Robert Elliott, congressman from South Carolina, debated with Alexander Stephens, one-time vice president of the Confederate States. Stephens, a white-haired shrunken figure in a wheel chair, opposed a bill that would ban discrimination against

Southern classroom

Negroes in public places. Elliott, broad-shouldered, young and handsome, spoke in favor of the bill.

As word of the debate between "the Anglo-Saxon and the African" flew around Capitol Hill, spectators jammed the galleries. Elliott gave a moving two-hour speech, answering Stephens' arguments and defending the rights of all citizens to equal justice. He sat down to wild applause. Congressmen crowded around to shake his hand, while reporters hurried to the telegraph office to wire the text of his speech to their papers. A year later, in 1875, Congress passed a Civil Rights Act which stated that "Citizens of every race and color" were entitled "to equal enjoyment of the accommodations of inns, public conveyances on land and water, theaters and other places of public amusement."

Across the South, Negroes and whites rode in the same streetcars and trains, ate in the same restaurants and soda fountains and, in some cities, sent their children to the same schools. Negro fathers chopping cotton in the fields and Negro mothers carrying scrub pails began to dream of "my son the lawyer," "my daughter the teacher." When a black boy in a Georgia classroom was asked what message he would like to send to children in the North, his answer was, "Tell 'em we're rising."

During the first days of reconstruction, a reporter called the freedmen's participation in government "the most incredible, hopeful and unbelievable experiment in all the history of mankind." It was an experiment that was bound to fail. The ex-slaves had won a share of political power but their old masters still had the upper hand. They owned the land—and the guns.

"IN THE HURRY AND CONFUSION OF THE HOUR, AND
THE EAGER DESIRE TO HAVE THE UNION RESTORED,
THERE WAS MORE CARE FOR THE SUBLIME SUPERSTRUCTURE
OF THE REPUBLIC THAN FOR THE SOLID
FOUNDATION UPON WHICH IT COULD ALONE BE UPHELD.
TO THE FREEDMEN WAS GIVEN THE MACHINERY OF
LIBERTY, BUT THERE WAS ALSO DENIED TO THEM
THE STEAM TO PUT IT INTO MOTION. THEY WERE
GIVEN THE UNIFORM OF SOLDIERS, BUT NO ARMS;
THEY WERE CALLED CITIZENS, BUT LEFT SUBJECTS;
THEY WERE CALLED FREE, BUT LEFT ALMOST SLAVES."

Frederick Douglass, 1880

"IF I VOTES THE REPUBLICAN TICKET, I WAKES
UP IN THE MORNING IN A GRAVEYARD."

A Negro, 1880

CHAPTER 8

A Dream Betrayed

Forty Acres . . .

After General William T. Sherman captured Savannah in the last months of the war he summoned a group of Negroes to his headquarters. In an interview that continued until "the small hours of the morning," he asked them to "state in what manner you think you can take care of yourselves and how you can best assist the Government in maintaining your freedom."

"The way we can best take care of ourselves," an ex-slave replied, "is to have land, and till it by our labor. We want to be placed on land until we are able to buy it, and make it our own."

The general listened thoughtfully. He was faced with the problem of finding food and shelter for more than ten thousand Negroes who had fled from their owners as his troops marched through Georgia. At that moment, the federal government was the largest landowner in the South. A series of Confiscation Acts passed by Congress had given the army authority to take over the property of all "engaged in armed rebellion" against the United States. To these holdings were added plantations abandoned by their owners or seized for nonpayment of taxes.

Sherman was a hardheaded military man with no special sympathy for Negroes. But if land was what they needed to become independent, why not give it to them? Three days after the Savannah interview, he issued a special field order. The coastal lands from Charleston, South Carolina, to Jacksonville, Florida, were to be set aside for Negro farms. Each family was to receive "forty acres of tillable ground . . . to establish a peaceable agricultural settlement. The sole and exclusive management of affairs will be left to the freed peoples themselves, subject only to the United States military authority and the acts of Congress."

All during the spring and summer of 1865, black homesteaders flocked to the coast. Forty thousand freedmen received "possessory" titles to 485,000 acres of land. "We shall build our cabins and organize our town government for the maintenance of order," a minister told a newspaperman.

The reporter was impressed by what he saw. "He and his fellow-colonists selected their lots, laid out a village, numbered their lots, put the numbers in a hat, and drew them out. It was Plymouth colony repeating itself. They agreed if any others came to join them, they should have equal privileges. So blooms the Mayflower on the South Atlantic coast."

Homes were built, crops were planted and freedmen's aid societies helped set up schools. But the black "Plymouth colonies" did not last long. President Andrew Johnson began to issue pardons to the rebels and to order their confiscated property returned. Before the first harvest was in, the former owners were claiming the land.

At first the Negro farmers drove them away. "You had better go back to Charleston," one man shouted. "If you can do nothing else, you can pick oysters and earn your living as the loyal people have—by the sweat of their brows."

At first the officers of the Freedmen's Bureau who had been appointed to oversee the settlements, sided with the farmers. But when the rebels petitioned the President he ordered General Howard, the head of the Bureau, to work out a "mutually satisfactory" arrangement.

Meeting with the freedmen in a crowded church in South Carolina, General Howard tried to explain to them that they must give up their homes. Cries of "No, No!" interrupted him. "Why do you take away our lands?" a man called from the gallery. "You take them from us who have always been true to the government! You give them to our all-time enemies! That is not right!" When a woman sang "Nobody knows the trouble I feel—Nobody knows but Jesus," even Howard's eyes clouded with tears.

Thirteen months after General Sherman's field order, soldiers evicted the freedmen. They were ordered to sign work contracts with the ex-Confederates or leave. Some marched from the fields with their hoes on their shoulders, announcing their determination to "work for no rebels." For most, the choice was work or starve. They stayed on the plantations as laborers.

Similar black settlements elsewhere in the South met the same fate. At Davis Bend in Mississippi, General Grant had set aside six plantations, including those formerly owned by Jefferson Davis and his brother, as "a Negro paradise." Almost two thousand Negroes joined the Davis Bend colony. They raised and marketed their crops, pocketing substantial profits at the end of a season. But they too were driven from the land in 1866. Only on the Sea Islands of South Carolina where freedmen had bought farms during the war were they left in possession of the land.

Cotton plantation on the Mississippi, 1883

For a year, two years, the dream of forty acres and a mule to plow them still persisted. Negroes and their friends in Congress tried to convince the nation that giving farms to the freedmen was both just and wise. In 1861 when the Russian serfs were freed Tsar Alexander II had ordered their masters to settle them on land for which the peasants paid in yearly installments. And in Biblical times hadn't the Egyptians given silver and gold to the Jews when they left the land of bondage? Congressman Thaddeus Stevens reminded the House of this.

In speech after speech he pointed out that seventy thousand men in the South—1 per cent of the white population—owned almost 90 per cent of the land. If the estates of these "chief rebels" were broken up, the freedmen and the poor whites could have farms.

"Make them independent of their old masters, so that they may not be compelled to work for them upon unfair terms," Stevens urged. "The whole fabric of southern society *must* be changed, and never can it be done if this opportunity is lost."

The Congress that gave civil rights to the freedmen was unwilling to disturb property rights. The opportunity was lost and a hundred years later Negroes were still trying to change the fabric of southern society. Although some exceptional or lucky freedmen managed to buy land, the vast majority were at the mercy of their old masters.

"Feeling themselves entitled to our labor without the payment of wages, it was not strange that they should make the hardest bargains for our labor, and get it for as little as possible," Frederick Douglass said. "Their tremendous power and our weakness easily gave them the victory."

The "bargain" that most freedmen accepted was sharecropping. Instead of working for wages, they were to receive a share of the crop that they raised. The planter supplied tools and seed, a house of sorts and allowed the sharecropper to buy food on credit at his plantation store. Prices at the store were exorbitant. Ex-slaves paid sixty cents for a pound of bacon, thirty cents for a pound of sugar, two dollars for a gallon of molasses that would cost only twenty-five cents in a city market. After the crop was sold, these items were deducted from the cropper's share. With the planter keeping the records, the "deducts" usually added up to more than the share. At the end of a year's hard work, the cropper owed money to the planter. Since he couldn't repay it, he had to stay on the plantation for another year. Season after season, the debt grew until the sharecropper, his children and his children's children were chained to the land that was not their own.

The Invisible Empire

To control the fortunate few who became independent farmers or businessmen, the planters found other methods. On an April night in 1867 a group of men met at the Maxwell House, a hotel in Nashville, Tennessee, to form a secret southwide or-

Sharecropper's home

ganization—the Ku Klux Klan. Their purpose was "to regenerate our unfortunate country and to relieve the White Race from the humiliating condition to which it has lately been reduced. Our main and fundamental objective is the MAINTENANCE OF THE SUPREMACY OF THE WHITE RACE in this Republic."

Everything about the Klan was wrapped in mystery. Its members met at night, wearing white (or sometimes black) robes and hoods. At the local level they were organized into Dens led by a Grand Cyclops. Each county in which there were Dens was a Province under a Grand Giant, each state a Realm headed by a Grand Dragon, while a Grand Wizard ruled the Invisible Empire.

Behind the masquerade of comic-sounding titles and disguises, the Klan was deadly serious. The Grand Wizard chosen at the Maxwell House meeting was Nathan Bedford Forrest, a former slave trader and the Confederate general who had been in command at Fort Pillow, Arkansas, when more than three hundred Negro prisoners of war were massacred. Assisting him as Grand Dragons and Giants were other Confederate officers and Southerners of prominence who had obtained presidential pardons by swearing that they would never again oppose the federal government.

With their hoods concealing their faces, Klansmen roamed the countryside at night. Sometimes they fixed a WARNING! notice to a door with the tip of a dagger: "You must vacate Jerry Owens' place. He was run off and his house burnt and now you are building and improving it. When you leave set fire to all the buildings. You are marked and watched closely by the K.K.K."

More often they surrounded a house and dragged out its occupants. A husband, wife and all four children were whipped in Florida because the Klan did not allow "damned niggers to live on land of their own." Jourdan Ware, a Georgia farmer, "was doing well and was comfortable," according to a white witness. He was driven from his home because he made "an

Knight of the Ku Klux Klan

insulting remark to a white lady. He remarked, 'How d'ye do, sis?' as the young lady passed down the road. She was a sister of the lady from whom he had rented the place."

Alfred Richardson, a carpenter, was told, "You are making too much money and you control all the colored votes. We do not allow a nigger to rise that way." He was shot. So was Joe Kennedy after he married "a bright-colored woman." The Klan "did not intend he should marry so white a woman as she was. They beat her also for marrying so black a Negro as he was."

When Hannah Tutson refused to give up the land she had worked for three years to buy, Klansmen tied her to a tree, stripped her naked and beat her with saddle girths. "They whipped me from the crown of my head to the soles of my feet. I was just raw," she said.

"Dam' Your Soul. The Horrible *Sepulchre* and Bloody Moon has at last arrived. Some live to-day to-morrow "*Jie.*" We the undersigned understand through our Grand "*Cyclops*" that you have recommended a big Black Nigger for Male agent on our mi rode; wel, sir, Jest you understand in time if he gets on the rode you can make up your mind to pull roape. If you have any thing to say in regard to the Matter, meet the Grand Cyclops and Conclave at Den No. 4 at 12 o'clock midnight, Oct. 1st, 1871.

"When you are in Calera we warn you to hold your tounge and not speak so much with your mouth or otherwise you will be taken on supprise and led out by the Klan and learnt to stretch hemp. Beware. Beware. Beware. Beware.
    (Signed)   "PHILLIP ISENBAUM,
                                 "*Grand Cyclops.*
                           "JOHN BANKSTOWN.
                           "ESAU DAVES.
                           "MARCUS THOMAS.
                           "BLOODY BONES."
" You know who. And all others of the Klan."

Perry Jeffers, farmer, defended himself when the Klan paid him a visit. After his son killed a white-robed figure, the Klan decreed that all of the Jeffers men must die. They shot Jeffers and his four grown sons, cremated his youngest boy and hanged his wife.

Elias Hill, crippled since childhood, taught a school for colored children. He was also a preacher and a leader in the Republican Party in his district. Klansmen broke into his cabin one night and cut his shriveled legs with a horsewhip. "They said I must quit preaching and put a card in the newspaper renouncing Republicanism," he recalled. "If I did not they would come back and kill me."

Not all of the victims of Klan terror were black. Some were white men and women who taught in colored schools and in the Klan's opinion "wanted to make niggers equal to the white man." Others voted Republican. Since the Republican Party in the person of Abraham Lincoln had freed the slaves and Republican-controlled Congresses had passed the Fourteenth and Fifteenth Amendments, Klansmen looked on white Republicans as traitors.

James Justice, a member of the North Carolina legislature, was beaten for "supporting the Republican Party and advocating principles that gave Negroes the right to vote and hold office." John Genobles and Samuel F. White were whipped until they agreed to change their politics. Acting under Klan orders, Genobles stood on the courthouse steps in Spartanburg, South Carolina, and announced, "I am not in favor of a black Republican government. I think that a white man is somewhat superior to a black." White put a notice in *The Spartan*, a Democratic paper:

MR. EDITOR: *I desire to make this public announcement of my withdrawal from all affiliation with the Republican Party. I am prompted to take this step from conviction that the policy of said party, in encouraging fraud, bribery, and excessive taxation, is calculated to ruin the government.*

Respectfully, SAMUEL F. WHITE

His was one of forty-five such notices in *The Spartan* in a few months' time.

By 1868 the Invisible Empire reached everywhere in the South. A U. S. Army commander in Texas wrote, "The murder of Negroes is so common as to render it impossible to keep accurate accounts of them." Members of the Tennessee legislature said, "Murders, to say nothing of other outrages, average one a day." In Virginia officers of the Freedmen's Bureau reported, "The Ku Klux Klan have made their appearance, visiting the houses of colored men at night, in some cases placing ropes around their necks and threatening to hang them on account of their political opinions." In Arkansas, "Three churches belonging to the freedmen were burned by parties unknown." In Georgia, "Freedmen have been discharged and driven from their homes for voting contrary to the wishes of their employers. Murders are frequent; the abuse of the blacks is too common to excite notice."

A congressional committee investigating the 1868 elections in Louisiana wrote: "Over 2,000 persons were killed, wounded, and otherwise injured prior to the election. Midnight raids, secret murders, and open riot kept the people in constant terror until the Republicans surrendered all claims and the election was carried by the Democracy." In the parish of St. Landry alone "The Ku Klux killed and wounded over two hundred Republicans, hunting and chasing them for two days and nights through fields and swamps. A pile of 25 dead bodies was found half buried in the woods." In the previous election Republicans had a thousand-vote majority in St. Landry. After the Klan rode, not one Republican vote was cast.

Congress tried to halt the violence. A joint committee of the House and Senate spent ten months listening to testimony from Klan victims. Afterward they issued a thirteen-volume report that described murders, mutilations and whippings in sickening detail. Three separate laws were passed to protect the rights of voters and to punish persons who "shall conspire together, or go in disguise . . . for the purpose . . . of depriving any class of persons of the equal protection of the laws."

These laws were like an old recipe for bear stew that began, "First, catch the bear." The conspirators had to be arrested, given a jury trial and convicted in courts in the South. Few white men would testify against a Klansman or vote to find him guilty. Negroes knew that they were signing their death warrants if they did so.

The Ku Klux Acts, as they were called, gave the President power to declare martial law wherever state authorities were unable to keep order. During the fall elections in 1871 President Grant sent troops to nine South Carolina counties. Five hundred men were arrested and fifty-five given jail sentences. But the Attorney General whose job it was to bring the conspirators to trial estimated that there were ten times that many Klansmen in the area. "It is too much even for the United States to undertake to inflict adequate penalties through the courts," he wrote. "Really these combinations amount to war, and cannot be effectually crushed on any other theory."

The war spread. Klansmen, growing bolder, took off their hoods and rode by day. They were joined by White Leaguers, Pale Faces, Knights of the White Camelia, the White Brotherhood, the Red Shirts.

"Every Democrat," said the Red Shirts, "must feel honor bound to control the vote of at least one Negro, by intimidation, purchase, keeping him away. Never threaten a man individually. If he deserves to be threatened, the necessities of the times require that he should die."

Hundreds died. Thousands were intimidated. On election days, armed men patrolled the voting places. Democrats, voting "early and often," destroyed the ballots cast by Republicans. Negroes and their white allies did their share of gun toting and ballot stealing too, but they were outnumbered.

"We cannot hold a meeting without being molested. Our lives are not safe," black voters told the Republican governor of Mississippi. Each day his mail brought calls for help. "I beg you to send soldiers here. They have hung six more men. They won't let the Republican have no ticket. Send troops and arms pleas . . . The rebels turbulent. Are aiming now to murder more poor Negroes. Gov., aint there no pertiction?"

There wasn't. In 1875 the governor asked President Grant to send troops to police the election. Grant's Attorney General turned him down. "The whole public are tired of these annual autumnal outbreaks in the South," he said.

The nation was bored with the "worn-out cry of 'southern outrages,'" another politician added. The first killings and beatings had aroused northern sympathies but as the violence continued, people's feelings became blunted. Another hundred or so dead black men was just a statistic, to be noted in the morning paper and then forgotten.

Besides, the North was impatient with the long slow process of reconstructing the South. Businessmen wanted to build railroads and factories and invest money in southern real estate. "As merchants we want to see the South gain her normal condition in the commerce of the country," a New York Republican explained. He thought that it had been a mistake to make the freedmen feel "that the United States government was their special friend, rather than those among whom they must live and for whom they must work. We have tried this long enough. Now let the South alone."

Good-by

After the election of 1876, President Hayes announced a hands-off policy. U.S. troops were withdrawn and brigades of Red Shirts and White Leaguers installed Democratic governors in all the states of the old Confederacy. Negro lawmakers were expelled from the legislatures, Negro sheriffs and policemen were disarmed, Negro judges and jurors dismissed.

Not all at once. Negroes had pockets of power in "black counties" where they were in the majority. But whites still tried to prevent them from voting or counted out the ballots

they cast. At last even the White Leaguers grew tired of
"the annual autumnal outbreaks" on Election Day.

"Cheating at elections is demoralizing our whole people,"
a Virginian said. "We have been stuffing ballot boxes, com-
mitting perjury and carrying the elections by fraud," a Mississippi judge declared. "No man can be in favor of perpetuating
the election methods which have prevailed since 1875 who is
not a moral idiot. The old men of the present generation can't
afford to die and leave their children with shot guns in their
hands, a lie in their mouths and perjury on their souls in
order to defeat the Negroes," another Mississippian believed.

To Negroes, the solution for troubled consciences seemed
obvious—hold honest elections with "freedom of ballot for all."
But white Southerners chose a different remedy. To eliminate
fraud and violence they decided to eliminate Negro voting—
by law.

Legislators searched for a way to say, "Black man, stay
home." They couldn't say it openly because that would defy
the Fifteenth Amendment. Nor could they set up educational
or property requirements for voters without keeping illiterate
and poor whites from the polls.

Mississippi found the answer in 1890 when it wrote a new
constitution. In addition to a poll tax which sharecroppers
would find difficult to pay, the law required a voter to "read
any section of the constitution or to be able to understand
the same when read to him, or give a reasonable interpretation
thereof." On its face the law did not violate the Fifteenth
Amendment, but everyone knew what it meant. Any white man,
no matter how ignorant, would be able to "understand" the
constitution. Any Negro, no matter how educated, would fail
the test.

"There's no particle of fraud or illegality in it," Senator
Benjamin Tillman said when South Carolina wrote its own
"understanding clause" five years later. "It's just simply showing partiality, perhaps, or discriminating."

Louisiana followed with a "grandfather clause" which allowed

"One Vote Less"

a man to vote without taking a literacy test if his father or grandfather had been a voter on January 1, 1867. Since no Negro had been eligible to vote then, the clause offered another loophole for white illiterates. In quick succession North Carolina, Alabama, Virginia, Georgia took over these devices or invented "good character clauses" that served the same purpose.

Black men stayed home. The Supreme Court found the "grandfather clause" unconstitutional in 1915 but the "understanding clause" kept most Negroes from voting in the Deep South until 1965.

Twenty-two black Southerners served in Congress in the years after the Civil War. In 1901 George H. White of North Carolina, the last Negro congressman from the South, rose on the floor of the House to say good-by:

"This, Mr. Chairman, is the Negroes' temporary farewell to the American Congress. He will rise up some day and come again. These parting words are in behalf of an outraged, heart-broken, bruised and bleeding, but God-fearing people, faithful, industrious, loyal people—rising people, full of potential force . . . I am pleading for the life, liberty, the future happiness, and manhood suffrage of one-eighth of the entire population of the United States."

North Carolina lawmakers celebrated the end of White's term with speeches of thanksgiving. Across the country, Negroes wept.

"THEY TELL US WE ARE FREE; THAT WE ARE CITIZENS;
THAT WE ARE UNDER THE PROTECTION OF THE LAW.
IT'S A LIE, FOR THE BLIND GODDESS RAISES HER BANDAGE
FROM THE EYES TO ASCERTAIN THE RACE AND COLOR
OF THOSE KNEELING AT HER SHRINE BEFORE SHE DISPENSES LAW.
AND WHEN WE MURMUR, COMPLAIN, CRY ALOUD AND DEMAND
OUR CONSTITUTIONAL RIGHTS AND PRIVILEGES, THEY TELL US
WE ARE DRAWING THE COLOR LINE. IT IS FALSE.
THE WHITE MAN DRAWS THE COLOR LINE."

E. J. Waring, Negro lawyer and founder of
The Mutual United Brotherhood of Liberty, Baltimore, 1887

CHAPTER 9

The Birth of Jim Crow

Following the Election Returns

Negroes had lost the land they had dreamed of owning. They had lost the right to vote and hold public office. Now they watched the last of their civil rights disappear.

In 1883 five men and women asked the Supreme Court for help. Bird Gee had been refused service in a Kansas restaurant because he was a Negro. Sallie Robinson had been evicted from the first-class car of a train in Tennessee because she was a Negro. W. H. R. Agee had been turned away from a Missouri hotel because he was a Negro. William Davis and George Tyler had been denied seats in New York and San Francisco theaters because they were Negroes. All five claimed that the rights granted them by the Civil Rights Act of 1875 had been violated.

It is the duty of the Supreme Court, as the highest court in the land, to decide whether state and federal laws are in conflict with the Constitution. While the justices are expected to make impartial decisions based solely on points of law they are, nevertheless, men who cannot always avoid being influenced by the atmosphere of their day. Although they do not decide a case by taking a public opinion poll, they have sometimes been accused of "following the election returns."

In 1883 "the election returns" were clear. The nation's concern for Negro rights was ebbing fast. It was more than a question of letting the South alone. The fact that four of these five cases came from the North and West showed that prejudice was rising everywhere.

Few political leaders were surprised when the Supreme Court decided that the Civil Rights Act of 1875 was unconstitutional. The Fourteenth Amendment, the justices said, prohibited states from discriminating but said nothing about "the wrongful act of an individual." "Inns, public conveyances, and places of amusement" were free to make their own rules. The complaints of Bird Gee and the others had no legal standing.

John Marshall Harlan of Kentucky, the Court's only Southerner, disagreed. As a slaveowner, Harlan had opposed emancipation and equal rights. He had changed his mind during the reconstruction years, as he watched Kentucky Negroes work, vote and become useful citizens. Now he not only believed in the brotherhood of man, but he knew, better than his fellow justices, that federal protection was needed if Negroes were to have an equal chance in the South.

In his lonely dissent, Harlan pointed out that "inns, public conveyances, and places of amusement" were not private individuals. They were licensed by state and local governments to serve the public—and "the colored race is part of that public." If Congress was not allowed to pass laws to strengthen the Fourteenth Amendment, he foresaw a time when "the rights of freedom and American citizenship" would not receive "that efficient protection which was unhesitatingly accorded to slavery and the rights of the master."

Although most newspapers praised the Court's decision, Negroes were stunned. John Mercer Langston, who had become U. S. Minister to Haiti, called it "a stab in the back." Frederick Douglass found it "one more shocking development of moral weakness in high places." Colored people felt as if they had been "baptised in ice water," wrote T. Thomas Fortune, editor of the New York *Globe*. He proposed that Negroes refuse to move from first-class coaches on trains. If they were killed, it would be for a good cause. "One or two murders growing from this intolerable nuisance would break it up," he said.

Conventions of Negroes campaigned so vigorously that almost all of the northern and midwestern states passed laws forbidding discrimination in public places. But the Court's decision left the South free to move in the opposite direction.

Homer Plessy Goes to Court

On June 7, 1892, Homer Adolph Plessy walked into the New Orleans railroad station and bought a first-class ticket to Covington, Louisiana. Plessy, a light-skinned man who described himself as having "one-eighth African blood" had no intention of going to Covington, however. His destination was jail.

Two years earlier the Louisiana legislature had passed "An Act to promote the comfort of passengers." The law required railroads "to provide equal but separate accommodations for the white and colored races." With the backing of the *Crusader*, a local paper, New Orleans Negroes had organized a Citizens Committee to Test the Constitutionality of the Separate Car Law. Funds were raised, lawyers hired, and Plessy volunteered to make the test.

Climbing aboard the train, he took a seat in the coach reserved for whites. The conductor ordered him to move to the "colored" car. Perhaps Plessy's heart beat a little faster.

Perhaps the summer heat made his forehead damp. But no violence followed his refusal to move. The train was held at the station until a detective arrived to arrest him.

Brought to trial before Judge John Ferguson a few days later, Plessy and the Citizens Committee lawyers claimed that the Louisiana law violated the Thirteenth and Fourteenth Amendments. After they lost in the state courts, the case of Plessy *vs.* Ferguson began its long slow trip to Washington.

The case was argued in April 1896. On May 18, Plessy and his lawyers went to the old Supreme Court Chamber in the Capitol to hear the justices' ruling. Thirteen years had passed since the death of the Civil Rights Act. The condition of the Negro in the South had gone from bad to much worse. Nine states had laws similar to Louisiana's and two were already using the "understanding clause" to keep black voters from the polls. Would the Court again "follow the election returns"?

Plessy leaned forward as Judge Henry B. Brown read the seven-to-one majority decision:

"The object of the [fourteenth] amendment was undoubtedly to enforce the absolute equality of the two races before the law but it could not have been intended to abolish distinctions based on color or to enforce . . . a commingling of the two races upon terms unsatisfactory to either." The Louisiana law was "a reasonable regulation" that "neither abridges the privileges of the colored man, deprives him of his property, nor denies him the equal protection of the laws, within the meaning of the Fourteenth Amendment."

Homer Plessy had lost his case. He could take cold comfort from the opinion of Justice Harlan, again the only judge to dissent. In words that later became famous, Harlan declared, "Our Constitution is color-blind and neither knows nor tolerates classes among citizens. In respect of civil rights, all citizens are equal before the law.

"If a State can prescribe that whites and blacks shall not travel in the same railroad coach, why may it not punish whites and blacks who ride together in street cars or in open vehicles on a public road?" he asked. "Why may it not require sheriffs to assign whites to one side of a courtroom and blacks to the other? And why may it not also prohibit the commingling of the two races in public assemblages?

"We boast of the freedom enjoyed by our people above all other peoples. But it is difficult to reconcile that boast with a law which, practically, puts the brand of servitude and degradation upon a large class of our fellow-citizens. The thin disguise of 'equal' accommodations for passengers in railroad coaches will not mislead anyone, nor atone for the wrong this day done."

Despite Harlan's warning that "the judgment rendered will, in time, prove to be quite as pernicious as the decision in the Dred Scott case," the Court's decision created little stir. The New York *Times* gave it a few lines on page 3, misspelling Plessy's name, and other papers failed to mention it at all.

Homer Plessy and his friends walked down the Capitol steps with stony faces. The court had put its stamp of approval on "separate but equal." The wrong done on that May day in 1896 would take more than a half century to set right.

The Wall

During the next years, all of Justice Harlan's predictions came true. Across the South, whites and blacks were separated in streetcars, steamboats, taxi cabs. Separate coaches on trains were followed by separate waiting rooms and ticket windows. Sheriffs assigned whites to one side of a courtroom and blacks to the other—and provided separate Bibles for witnesses of the two races to swear on.

That was only the beginning. Whites and blacks were forbidden to mingle in theaters and concert halls. Circuses had "colored" entrances. Ball parks had separate bleachers and

white and Negro teams were no longer allowed to play against each other. Bars that had formerly served both races were partitioned, with whites drinking at the upper end and Negroes at the lower. Then laws required separate "white" and "colored" bars, separate hotels and restaurants. And separate orphanages, old-age homes, insane asylums.

Prisoners were separated in jails, the sick in hospitals. Only "colored" ambulances were allowed to pick up colored patients. Only colored nurses took care of them. At death they were carried off in a "colored" hearse and buried in a "colored" cemetery.

Trees in city parks sprouted signs: NO NEGROES AL-
LOWED. Drinking fountains in villages squares had separate
WHITE and COLORED faucets. WHITES ONLY was painted
on windows of barber shops, laundries, billiard parlors. Office
buildings had two elevators, one labeled PASSENGERS, the
other FOR NEGROES AND FREIGHT.

Cities, counties, states seemed to compete with each other
to find new areas that could be segregated. Kentucky and
North Carolina ruled that "no textbook issued to a colored
child shall ever be re-issued to a white child." Florida went
further by requiring schoolbooks to be separated even in ware-
houses. Virginia banned fraternities or clubs where Negroes
and whites addressed each other as "brother." After telephones
became common, Oklahoma ordered the telephone company
"to maintain separate booths for white and colored patrons."
When cotton mills were built in South Carolina, black and
white mill hands were prohibited from working in the same
room, using the same staircase, or looking out of the same
window!

The segregation laws were called Jim Crow laws, after a blackface comedian who had done a "Jim Crow" dance in an old-time minstrel show. They established separation but never equality. Jim Crow cars on trains were soot-filled coaches, used for baggage as well as passengers. The whole front of a railroad station was assigned to white people. Negroes had a side entrance and a tiny waiting room in the rear. Whites sat in the orchestra in theaters; Negroes walked through an alley to climb to the balcony.

Jimmy Crow

Negro children in particular were shortchanged. In the first years of the twentieth century, public libraries were built—for whites only. A few cities opened small branch libraries for Negroes but as late as 1929 there were only twenty in all of the southern states. Most parks were "off limits." So were public beaches, swimming pools, playgrounds, amusement parks.

"Out of every dollar of the state school money," a Georgia Equal Rights Convention reported in 1906, "eighty cents go to the white child and twenty to the Negro." Ten years later South Carolina spent $12.37 on each white student, $1 for each Negro in the state. "Colored" schools were often open for only two or three months a year and seldom went beyond fourth grade. Twenty years after the Plessy *vs.* Ferguson decision, there were no more than sixty-four public high schools for Negroes in the entire South, and no public medical or law schools.

Wherever a black boy turned, a wall labeled WHITES ONLY blocked him off.

The Compromise

The birth of Jim Crow brought forward a new kind of Negro spokesman. Booker T. Washington was nine when the Thirteenth Amendment set him free. Educated at Hampton Institute in Virginia, he went to Alabama in 1881 to start a school at Tuskegee. Life in rural Alabama convinced him that the struggle for equal rights was hopeless. Temporarily at least, Negroes must learn to live as second-class citizens and raise themselves by thrift and hard work.

When he was asked to speak at the Cotton States Exposition in Atlanta in 1895, Washington proposed a compromise to the South. He called on Negroes to forget civil rights. "The

Booker T. Washington

opportunity to earn a dollar in a factory just now is worth infinitely more than the opportunity to spend a dollar in an opera house," he said. "In all things that are purely social we can be as separate as the fingers, yet one as the hand in all things essential to mutual progress."

In return for accepting Jim Crow, he asked his white listeners to give Negroes jobs and schools. "With education of head, hand and heart you will find that they will buy your surplus land, make blossom the waste places in your fields, and run your factories. While doing this you can be sure," he promised, "that you and your families will be surrounded by the most patient, faithful, law-abiding and unresentful people that the world has seen."

Washington's compromise made him a national figure overnight. Northerners and Southerners sighed with relief and praised his statesmanship. Now "the race question" could be forgotten and the South could get on with its long-postponed plans to industrialize. "Your words cannot fail to delight all who wish well for your race," wrote President Cleveland. "If our colored citizens do not gather new hope, it will be strange indeed."

For twenty years, Booker T. Washington was the most powerful black man in America. The country schoolmaster became the advisor to Presidents and the honored guest of rich northern industrialists. During the presidencies of Theodore Roosevelt and William Taft, no Negro received a federal appointment unless Washington okayed it. Although the South failed to support Negro schools, men like John D. Rockefeller and Andrew Carnegie placed millions of dollars for education in Washington's hands.

Nevertheless, Washington's compromise failed. Before his death in 1915, he was under attack for "leading the way backward." Tuskegee Institute and the other schools that he helped to establish were unlike the universities of Mississippi and South Carolina. Their goal, as Washington saw it, was to "make the Negro humble, simple, and of service to the community."

Cooking class at Tuskegee Institute

Instead of college subjects, black students were taught to work with their hands. Boys learned to farm, shoe horses, mend harnesses, bake bricks. Girls studied housekeeping, sewing, nursing and the making of brooms and mattresses. Tuskegee turned out a creditable number of hard-working, polite, neatly-dressed graduates, but the trades they had learned were nineteenth century trades while the nation was moving into the age of the factory assembly line, the Model T Ford, and the airplane.

Perhaps it wouldn't have mattered anyway, for the South didn't keep its side of the bargain. Factories were built but Negroes were employed there only as janitors. And planters held onto their land, refusing to sell it to Tuskegee graduates.

"It's a question who will do the dirty work," an Alabama lawyer explained. "In this country the white man won't. The Negro must. Educate him and he quits the field. Instruct him in the trades and sciences and he enters into active competition with the white man. That competition brings on friction, and that friction in the end means the Negro's undoing."

Senator Benjamin Tillman of South Carolina put it more directly: "If you want to rise, keep the nigger down!"

In the first years of the twentieth century, more than a hundred Negroes were lynched annually, many for the crime of being "uppity." These mob murders were unbelievably savage affairs. Some were announced ahead of time in newspapers so that men, women and children could turn out to watch the victim being roasted to death over a slow fire. Tuskegee kept a record of the lynchings, but little could be done to stop them. Since Negroes had lost all political power in the South, the occasional lyncher who was brought to trial was never convicted.

The Jim Crow wall grew higher. In its shadow, Negroes were forced to live in separate communities of their own. Black teachers taught black children, black ministers preached on Sundays, and there were black barbershops, insurance companies, funeral parlors. By walking humbly in the presence of their white neighbors, and remembering to use back doors and side entrances, some Tuskegee graduates managed to build up small businesses.

Others fled to the North.

"I'VE WATCHED THE TRAINS AS THEY DISAPPEARED
BEHIND THE CLOUDS OF SMOKE,
CARRYING THE CROWDS OF WORKING MEN
TO THE LAND OF HOPE . . .
YES, WE ARE GOING TO THE NORTH!
I DON'T CARE WHAT STATE,
JUST SO I CROSS THE DIXON LINE,
FROM THIS SOUTHERN LAND OF HATE . . ."

William Crosse in the Chicago Defender

CHAPTER 10

The Black Ghetto

The Exodusters

The dark days after reconstruction saw the first mass migration of Negroes from the South. Led by Benjamin Singleton who had been a conductor on the Underground Railroad and Henry Adams, a Civil War veteran, families took passage on Mississippi River boats, heading North. Singleton, who called himself "the Moses of the colored exodus," dreamed of founding black settlements on the plains of Kansas. Some of his "exodusters" reached Kansas to build sod huts and plant wheat on the bleak prairies. Most were stranded along the way. With their last dollars gone for steamship tickets, they shivered and starved in the river cities of Missouri and Illinois.

Negroes continued to drift northward but the next big exodus took place during World War I. The boll weevil, a beetle from Mexico, invaded the South's cotton fields at the same time that the war halted immigration from Europe. Northern factory owners were hungry for workers and southern sharecroppers were hungry, period. The *Chicago Defender*, a Negro paper that circulated in the South, filled its pages with news and letters similar to the "America letters" that Irish immigrants had once sent home.

". . . I work in the Swift Packing Co. in the sausage department. We get $1.50 a day and the hours are not so long . . . I make $90 a month with ease . . . I have saved enough to bring my wife and four children . . . Work is plenty here and we don't loaf . . . I am well and thankful to be in a city with no lynching and no beating . . ."

Special trains filled with "exodusters" left New Orleans, Birmingham, Memphis. The sides of the cars were covered with chalked slogans: FAREWELL—WE'RE GOOD AND GONE, BOUND FOR THE PROMISED LAND. So many thousands left that alarmed planters tried to halt the trains and sheriffs jailed men with copies of the *Defender* in their pockets. But the exodus continued.

Half a million black men and women moved to northern cities in the years between 1910 and 1920. Another three quarters of a million came in the next decade—and more are still coming.

In the "promised land" these country folk from the South were the greenhorns. Like the immigrants from Europe, they crowded into already crowded tenements and set up their own storefront churches and social clubs. As long as the war boom lasted, they found jobs in munitions factories, in the stockyards, on the docks. Afterward they worked as elevator operators, janitors, cafeteria workers—the least skilled jobs with the longest hours and the lowest pay.

Based on the immigrant experience, the migrants should have been able to climb up the economic ladder in a generation or two. They might even have been expected to move a little faster than the foreign-born for they were not really newcomers. They spoke the same language and shared the same history as the older residents of the cities. But there was an important difference between the migrants from the South and the European immigrants. The migrants' skins were black.

When they tried to climb the economic ladder, they found that all but its bottom rung was missing. Some industries barred them entirely. Others hired them for blind-alley jobs that did not lead to advancement or for work so unpleasant that white men were unwilling to accept it. A Negro could not sell goods in a store, but he could deliver them after they were sold. He could be a Pullman porter, but never a conductor or engineer. He could work at the blast furnace in a steel mill, handling white-hot metal "because the Negro is especially adapted to hot work." In an auto plant, he could spray paint on car bodies because "this soon kills a white man."

The opportunities open to white women to become secretaries, clerks, telephone operators, saleswomen were closed to Negroes. "No matter how intelligent or bright a Negro girl is, nobody wants a Negro stenographer," a teacher in a business school said.

Wherever Negroes worked they were paid less than whites. Want ads in New York newspapers after the war called for "FACTORY HELPERS. Experienced only. White $24, Colored $20." Employers were not the only ones to discriminate. In 1890 the American Federation of Labor had looked "with disfavor upon trade unions having provisions which exclude from membership persons on account of race or color." But ten years later Samuel Gompers, president of the AF of L and himself an immigrant, suggested that Negroes be organized in separate unions. By 1910 he opposed Negro union members because they could not "understand the philosophy of human rights."

Exclusion from unions kept Negroes from well-paid jobs as electricians, plasterers, painters, plumbers, although some had come from the South with a lifetime of experience in the building trades. Since most unions ran apprenticeship programs for young people, the sons of the Negro migrants—and their grandsons—were prevented from learning these skills.

Before World War I when the number of Negroes in northern cities was small, they enjoyed a fair degree of equality in their daily life. State civil rights laws forbade discrimination in restaurants and theaters. Although the laws were violated, they were still on the books and there was hope for better enforcement in the future.

In New York, Chicago, Cleveland, Negro neighborhoods were scattered throughout the cities. Most families grouped themselves together on "Negro blocks." Little Africa was across the street from Little Italy, around the corner from Polack Alley. "Where the Negro pitches his tent," a newspaperman wrote in 1902, "he pays more rent than his white neighbor next door and is a better tenant."

Negroes complained that "foreigners learn how to cuss, count and say 'nigger' as soon as they get here," but in the rough give and take of city life, they did their share of name calling too. Rival gangs of boys fought on the crowded streets, but everyone went to the same school. The residents of Little Africa were as free to move "uptown" as were the residents of Little Italy. All that they needed was rent money.

Pittsburgh slum

They Shall Not Pass!

This live-and-let-live attitude changed abruptly when large numbers of "exodusters" arrived. As the Negro population of cities doubled and tripled, whites began to talk of "black hordes" "invading" their neighborhoods. A huge banner across South Parkway at Forty-third Street in Chicago proclaimed, THEY SHALL NOT PASS! The words were the then familiar slogan of the French Army, fighting heroically to turn back the Germans. On South Parkway they were a warning to black Americans. Richard B. Harrison—later famous for his portrayal of the Lord in the play and film, *Green Pastures*—ignored the warning. When he moved beyond the boundary line, a bomb splintered his porch and shattered his front windows. Three bombs later the Harrisons were still there. They had no other place to go.

In New York, a newspaper printed scare headlines: BLACK INVADERS CAPTURE WHITE FLAT. "Drive them out!" a homeowner shouted. "Send them to the slums where they belong."

There was no more room in the slums. With Little Africas bursting at the seams, the newcomers moved into Harlem, one of the city's better residential neighborhoods. Harlem's white property owners met to find ways "to fight the common enemy." They discussed building a twenty-four-foot high fence to separate their streets from those where Negroes lived. They signed agreements, known as restrictive covenants, in which they promised not to sell or rent "to colored tenants or all persons of African descent." When Negro families moved nearby they broke their agreements. "In a rather panicky state of mind" they sold their homes and fled.

Harlem street

Real estate dealers, including some black men, did everything they could to cause this kind of panic. Then they bought the buildings at low prices and charged high rates to Negroes. The white homeowners lost, the Negro tenants lost and the real estate men made big profits.

In the 1920s Harlem became almost all black, leaving the rest of New York almost all white. While landlords in other parts of the city refused to rent to the migrants who were still flooding in from the South, landlords in Harlem welcomed them—and doubled the rent. By 1927, Negroes were paying ten dollars more a month for a four-room apartment than other New Yorkers and earning twenty-two dollars less.

"What you gonna do when the rent comes 'round?" an old Negro song asked. Harlem tenants took in lodgers. A four-room apartment housed two families. When times were bad, as they were in the '30s, three families and even four moved in together.

Then landlords discovered that they could make more money by subdividing the larger apartments and renting separate rooms. Mr. Jones, for instance, might own a building with six apartments. Each apartment had five rooms, a kitchen and bath and rented for forty dollars a month. When he rented by the room, charging twenty dollars a room, he collected six hundred dollars a month, two and a half times his former income.

Meanwhile, five families shared one kitchen and bath. Five times as much garbage was put out at night. Five times as many children ran up and down the stairs and attended the local school.

Harlem became unbelievably crowded. On one city block, 3871 people lived—something of a world record for congestion. Other records were set as well. Twice as many Harlem mothers were dying in childbirth as mothers in other parts of town. Harlem's rate for tuberculosis deaths became almost three times as high as the city-wide rate and the incidence of rickets, diphtheria and pneumonia was also higher among Harlem children.

As the houses bulged with people, landlords stopped taking care of them. Pipes leaked, plaster fell from the ceilings, light bulbs burned out in the halls. Rats and roaches had a population explosion of their own.

The city lost interest too. Harlem's streets were cleaned less often than Park Avenue, a few blocks south. Harlem's garbage was allowed to spill over into the alleys. Harlem Hospital was nicknamed "The Butcher Shop" because of the poor quality of its medical services—and no Negro doctors were allowed to work there. Instead of building more schools, the Board of Education packed the newcomers into those that were already there. Harlem schools had double or triple sessions, with forty to fifty pupils in a room—and teachers asked to be transferred to other sections of the city.

Before long every big city had its Harlem. A Chicago newspaper described "the fine network of contracts that like a marvelous delicately woven chain of armor" protected white neighborhoods. "And of what does this armor consist? It consists of a contract which the owner of the property signs not to exchange with, sell to, or lease to any member of a race not Caucasian." By 1930 three quarters of Chicago's homeowners had signed restrictive covenants or had unwritten "gentleman's agreements" not to sell to "undesirables."

If a Negro managed to break through the armor, he faced at the least name calling, often violence, sometimes death. In Chicago, fifty-eight Negro homes were bombed between 1917 and 1921. Two people were killed, dozens injured, and no one was punished for the bombings.

Negro families no longer migrated from Mississippi to Chicago. They went only to Chicago's South Side. In Boston they settled in Roxbury, in Detroit in Paradise Valley. The old mixed neighborhoods where Negroes and whites had lived across the street from one another disappeared. They were replaced by black ghettos.

The word "ghetto" comes from sixteenth-century Italy where Pope Paul IV decreed that "Jews shall live entirely separated

from Christians, in a quarter or a street with one entrance and exit." The Jewish quarter, which Venetians named a ghetto, had high walls separating it from the rest of the city. At night its heavy gate was locked and only Jews with special passes were allowed outside.

America's black ghettos separated people because of their color rather than their religion. Negroes could not move "uptown" even if they had the rent money. They were walled in by restrictive covenants and gentleman's agreements. Real estate brokers pledged not to show them homes outside of "colored districts." Banks refused to give them mortgages. After the Federal Housing Administration was established in 1934, even this government agency opposed "inharmonious racial groups" and supplied model restrictive covenants for home buyers to sign.

The South kept Negro citizens in "their place" with Jim Crow laws. The North used gentleman's agreements. The walls of the ghetto are invisible, but they are high, nevertheless. For a half century Negroes have struggled to destroy them.

"SOME GOOD FRIENDS OF THE CAUSE WE REPRESENT FEAR
AGITATION. THEY SAY: 'DO NOT AGITATE—DO NOT
MAKE A NOISE; WORK.' THEY ADD: 'AGITATION IS
DESTRUCTIVE OR AT BEST NEGATIVE—WHAT IS WANTED
IS POSITIVE CONSTRUCTIVE WORK.'
SUCH HONEST CRITICS MISTAKE THE FUNCTION OF
AGITATION. A TOOTHACHE IS AGITATION. IS A
TOOTHACHE A GOOD THING? NO. IS IT THEREFORE
USELESS? NO. IT IS SUPREMELY USEFUL, FOR IT TELLS
THE BODY OF DECAY AND DEATH. WITHOUT IT THE
BODY WOULD SUFFER UNKNOWINGLY. IT WOULD THINK:
ALL IS WELL, WHEN LO! DANGER LURKS."

W. E. B. Du Bois in The Crisis, *1910*

CHAPTER 11

Make Way for Democracy!

We Are Men

"Courage, brothers! The battle for humanity is not lost or losing. The morning breaks over blood-stained hills. We must not
falter, we may not shrink. Above are the everlasting stars."
    With these words, the modern civil rights movement was
born. The place was Harpers Ferry, West Virginia. At dawn on
August 18, 1906, one hundred men and women gathered in a
field outside of the fort where John Brown had made his stand
against slavery. As the slanting rays of the morning sun shone
on the fort, one of their number read an "Address to the
Country." The "Address" was both a declaration of independence from Booker T. Washington and a program for the
future:
    "We will not be satisfied to take one jot or tittle less than our

manhood rights. We claim for ourselves every single right that belongs to a free born American, political, civil and social. The battle we wage is not for ourselves alone, but for all true Americans. It is a fight for ideals, lest this, our common fatherland, false to its founding, become in truth the land of the thief and the home of the slave—a by-word and a hissing among the nations for its sounding pretentions and pitiful accomplishment.

"Our demands are clear. First, we would vote. We want full manhood suffrage, and we want it now, henceforth and forever.

"Second. We want discrimination in public accommodations to cease.

"Third. We claim the right of freemen to walk, talk and be with them that wish to be with us.

"Fourth. We want the laws enforced against rich as well as poor, against white as well as black.

"Fifth. We want our children educated. We want the national government to step in and wipe out illiteracy in the South. Either the United States will destroy ignorance or ignorance will destroy the United States. We want our children trained as intelligent human beings should be, and we will fight for all time against any proposal to educate black boys and girls simply as servants. They have a right to know, to think, to aspire.

"These are some of the chief things which we want. How shall we get them? By voting where we may vote, by persistent unceasing agitation, by hammering at the truth, by sacrifice and work.

"We refuse to surrender the leadership of this race to cowards and trucklers. We are men. We will be treated as men.

"And we shall win."

The author of the "Address" was William Edward Burghardt Du Bois. Poet and social scientist, Du Bois was born in Massachusetts in 1867 and was the first Negro to earn a Ph.D. from Harvard. Since 1897 he had been teaching at Atlanta University in Georgia. The harsh reality of life in a southern city drove him to oppose Washington's policy of compromise. A year earlier he had brought together a group of young Negroes. Meeting at Niagara Falls—on the Canadian side because U.S. hotels would not rent them rooms—they decided to fight for full citizenship rights. To dramatize the power that they hoped their organization would have, they named it the Niagara Movement.

The Niagara Movement continued to meet and to "hammer at the truth." Meanwhile thoughtful people across the country were troubled by riots that were occurring in the North as well as the South. For two days in 1908 a white mob took over the city of Springfield, Illinois, home of Abraham Lincoln. Shouting, "Lincoln freed you—we'll show you where you belong," they killed and wounded scores of Negroes and burned several blocks of homes. An eyewitness to the riot, William English Walling, reported on it in *The Independent*. Deeply concerned at what he had seen, he called for a revival of the old

W. E. B. Du Bois and the men of Niagara

antislavery spirit. "Yet who realizes the seriousness of the situation, and what large and powerful body of citizens is ready to come to their [the Negroes] aid?" he asked.

The body of citizens that came forward was neither large nor powerful but it included the leading liberals of the day: professors, social workers, newspapermen, ministers, rabbis, some of them descendants of the old abolitionists. On February 12, 1909, the one hundredth anniversary of Lincoln's birth, they proposed a national conference to renew "the struggle for civil and political liberty."

When the conference was held three months later in New York, the men of Niagara joined them. For the first time since reconstruction, Negroes and whites met together to plan a program for action.

"The debate was warm and even passionate," Dr. Du Bois wrote. "Impatience and anger appeared and out of all cropped suspicion. A woman leapt to her feet and cried in almost tearful earnestness—an earnestness born of bitter experience—'They are betraying us again—these white friends of ours.'

"But through all this the mass of the conference kept calm and good-natured. They were not certain of everything but they quietly voted through the plan of organization: a committee of forty and eventually a great central committee on the Negro problem, divided into carefully arranged and efficient departments of legal advice, social investigation, publicity, political propaganda and education."

In 1910 the committee of forty became the National Association for the Advancement of Colored People, soon known by its initials as the NAACP. Most of its officers were white but eight of the men of Niagara served on its first board of directors and W. E. B. Du Bois left Atlanta to become Director of Publicity and Research and editor of *The Crisis*, its monthly magazine.

The purpose of the NAACP as stated in its incorporation papers was "to promote equality of rights and eradicate race prejudice; to advance the interest of colored citizens; to secure

for them impartial suffrage; and to increase their opportunities for securing justice in the courts, education for their children, employment according to their ability and complete equality before the law."

The State Department

It was a big assignment. Fortunately the NAACP was able to share a part of it with another organization. In 1911 three groups interested in the problems of Negroes in New York joined to form the National League on Urban Conditions Among Negroes, later known as the National Urban League. Although today the Urban League is one of the "Big Five" of the civil rights movement, it did not start as a protest organization. Like the Italian Welfare League and the Hebrew Immigrant

Eugene Kinckle Jones

Aid Society, its concern was with the greenhorns pouring into the city who needed help in finding jobs, apartments and in adjusting to city ways. Most of the white members of the League's interracial board of directors were business executives. Its Negro staff people were economists and social workers.

In its early years, the Urban League was part travelers' aid society and part employment agency. Its slogan was "Not Alms but Opportunity." "We do not ask for charity," said Dr. William Lewis Bulkley, a school principal and the League's first vice-chairman. "All we ask is opportunity. We do not beg for alms. We beg only for a chance."

Through a "Negroes in Industry Week" or an "Equal Opportunity Day," the League tried to sell the idea of Negro workers to employers, unions and the public. It worked for jobs, more jobs and better jobs in fields then closed to Negroes. It also encouraged the training of Negro social workers, started Big Brother and Big Sister programs, opened day nurseries and health clinics and conducted house-to-house surveys of living conditions.

When the Urban League set up shop in New York with a staff of two and a budget of $8500, its goal, said executive secretary Eugene Kinckle Jones, was "to work itself out of a job." He looked forward to the time when Negroes would not be barred from employment or housing because of their color. However, the mushrooming growth of black ghettos increased the need for the Urban League. By the 1920s there were local leagues in thirty cities. Today eighty-four busy League offices spend more than six million dollars a year and find plenty of work that needs doing. Still an organization of professional social workers and volunteers rather than a mass membership group, the League builds bridges between Negroes and whites through community conferences and top-level meetings. One staff member described the Urban League as "the State Department of race relations" in contrast to the NAACP—"the War Department."

The War Department

Working out of a small rent-free office in downtown New York, the NAACP tried to cover all fronts at once. Mail poured in and the telephone rang continuously . . . A sharecropper in South Carolina sentenced to death . . . A workman lynched in Pennsylvania . . . Negro homes bombed in Kansas City . . . A Negro denied entrance to an amusement park in New Jersey . . . Negro firemen on the Southern Railway threatened with loss of their jobs . . . Negro lawyers excluded from the American Bar Association . . .

Meanwhile Du Bois plunged into *The Crisis*—"and soon there issued from it such clarity and sense, thunders of such wrath, and screeches of such derisive laughter that its audience of one thousand quickly grew to ten, then fifty, then one hundred thousand," said Saunders Redding, Negro novelist and critic. *The Crisis* was more than a news magazine. Alongside his angry

William Edward Burghardt Du Bois

eloquent editorials which were read and quoted by every literate Negro in the country, Du Bois printed poems, stories, plays by young Negro writers. At a time when the only pictures of Negroes that most people saw were insulting cartoons, *The Crisis* featured brown-skinned cover girls, distinguished Negro "Men of the Month" and serious high school and college students. Each issue said to its readers: "There is much injustice in the land. Fight—and be proud you are black!"

Before the NAACP had a chance to plan a long-range program Jim Crow cropped up in Washington, D.C. Since the Civil War, the federal government had been one of the few employers in the country that did not discriminate. Because government jobs were filled largely on the basis of civil service examinations, thousands of Negroes had found work in the capital. After the election of southern-born Woodrow Wilson, however, black clerks and stenographers were suddenly segregated.

In the post office the desks of colored clerks were moved to a corner, behind a row of lockers. The War Department ordered separate offices for Negro and white typists. WHITE and COLORED signs went up on rest rooms and Negroes were no longer permitted in the cafeterias in government buildings. At the same time, bills were introduced into Congress to legalize this segregation and to establish Jim Crow streetcars in the city.

The NAACP went into action. "Never before has the federal government discriminated against its civilian employees on the ground of color," its officers wrote in an open letter to the President. Congressmen were visited and Archibald Grimke, chairman of the Association's new Washington branch, testified before a House committee. "You cannot separate the colored people in the government service without humiliating them," Grimke said.

"Segregation is not humiliating but a benefit," Wilson replied to a delegation of Negro leaders.

When protests failed to move the President, the NAACP called a meeting that was attended by six thousand people—

the first civil rights mass meeting to be held in Washington. The bills in Congress were defeated but Wilson's segregation order remained in force for decades.

The outbreak of war in Europe found the NAACP divided. Some of its board members were pacifists, opposed to all wars. Others, believing that the Allies were fighting "to make the world safe for democracy," saw in the war a chance to broaden democracy at home. Board Chairman Joel Spingarn started a country-wide crusade to persuade the War Department to train Negro officers. His crusade succeeded except that the young men who volunteered for officers' training were sent to a separate Jim Crow camp. A second disappointment came when Colonel Charles Young, a West Point graduate and the highest-ranking Negro in the Army, was abruptly retired as "physically unfit." Young, who had been expected to take charge of the officers' camp, was only fifty-three years old. To prove his fitness he rode horseback from his home in Chillicothe, Ohio, to Washington—and was recalled to active duty to sit out the war with the Ohio National Guard.

Nevertheless, 639 Negroes were commissioned as captains and lieutenants. Du Bois, in what he later called "one of my periods of exaltation," wrote an editorial for *The Crisis* titled "Close Ranks." "Let us not hesitate. Let us, while this war lasts, forget our special grievances and close our ranks shoulder to shoulder with our own white fellow citizens. We make no ordinary sacrifice, but we make it gladly and willingly with our eyes lifted to the hills."

But it was hard to forget special grievances as reports of the mistreatment of Negro soldiers reached the NAACP office. Enlisted men in camps in the South were insulted and beaten. Sent overseas, they were given more than their share of mud slogging and less than their share of glory. Even the newly commissioned officers were treated with hate and scorn. Charles Houston, who later became dean of Howard University Law School and NAACP special counsel, wrote from France, "They boarded us off from our fellow white officers. They made us eat on benches in order to maintain segregation, and they destroyed our prestige in front of French officers."

At war's end, the NAACP sent Du Bois to France to investigate the charges and counter-charges. There he found a document called "Secret Information Concerning Black American Troops." Prepared at the request of the U. S. Army, it advised French officers not to treat Negroes as equals.

"The black man is regarded by the white American as an inferior being," the document said. "We must prevent the rise of any degree of intimacy between French officers and black officers . . . We must not commend too highly the black American troops, particularly in the presence of white Americans . . . Make a point of keeping the native population from 'spoiling' the Negroes . . ."

The Crisis printed the "Secret Information" along with an editorial addressed to the two hundred thousand black soldiers coming home from the war. "This country of ours, despite all its better souls have done and dreamed, is yet a shameful land. We return from fighting. We return fighting. Make way for Democracy! We saved it in France and, by the Great Jehovah, we will save it in the U.S.A. or know the reason why!"

That month *The Crisis* sold 125,000 copies and its editor was accused of "encouraging resistance" to the government. Agents of the Department of Justice visited the NAACP office.

"Just what is this organization fighting for?" a suspicious agent asked.

"We are fighting for the enforcement of the Constitution of the United States," Dr. Du Bois replied.

"THE RACE PROBLEM IN THE
UNITED STATES HAS RESOLVED
ITSELF INTO A QUESTION OF
SAVING BLACK MEN'S BODIES
AND WHITE MEN'S SOULS."

James Weldon Johnson, 1919

CHAPTER 12

The Shame of America

The Right to Live

From its first days, the NAACP had a map of the United States
hanging on its office wall. Pins were stuck into the map to mark
every town where a lynching had taken place. The map was
black with pins—and it grew blacker.

Seventy-eight Negroes were hanged, shot or burned alive the
year after the First World War. In addition to the lynchings,
the summer of 1919, which James Weldon Johnson, the
NAACP's executive secretary, called "The Red Summer," saw
more than two dozen race riots. In Texas, South Carolina,
Arkansas—and in Chicago, Omaha and Washington, D.C.—
white men attacked Negroes, shooting, beating and burning
their homes. The score of dead and wounded ran into the thousands.

Some of this violence could be traced to the Ku Klux Klan
which had been revived during the war. After a cross-burning
ceremony on Stone Mountain in Georgia, Imperial Wizard
William J. Simmons called on "native-born white Christians"
to preserve "the supremacy of the white race." The new Klan
was not only anti-Negro. For a ten-dollar initiation fee and
five dollars for a white robe and hood, a Klansman was

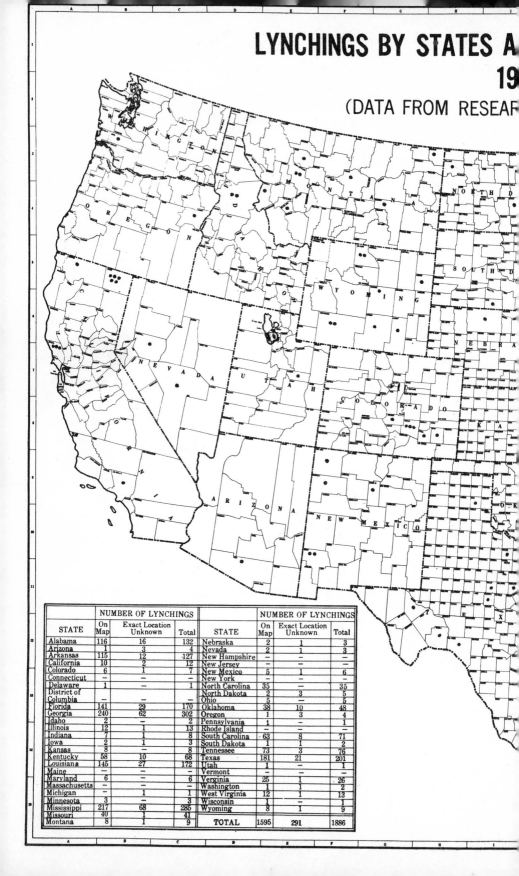

LYNCHINGS BY STATES A...
19...
(DATA FROM RESEAR...

STATE	NUMBER OF LYNCHINGS			STATE	NUMBER OF LYNCHINGS		
	On Map	Exact Location Unknown	Total		On Map	Exact Location Unknown	Total
Alabama	116	16	132	Nebraska	2	1	3
Arizona	1	3	4	Nevada	2	1	3
Arkansas	115	12	127	New Hampshire	–	–	–
California	10	2	12	New Jersey	–	–	–
Colorado	6	1	7	New Mexico	5	1	6
Connecticut	–	–	–	New York	–	–	–
Delaware	1	–	1	North Carolina	35	–	35
District of Columbia	–	–	–	North Dakota	2	3	5
Florida	141	29	170	Ohio	5	–	5
Georgia	240	62	302	Oklahoma	38	10	48
Idaho	2	–	2	Oregon	1	3	4
Illinois	12	1	13	Pennsylvania	1	–	1
Indiana	7	1	8	Rhode Island	–	–	–
Iowa	2	1	3	South Carolina	63	8	71
Kansas	8	–	8	South Dakota	1	1	2
Kentucky	58	10	68	Tennessee	73	3	76
Louisiana	145	27	172	Texas	181	21	201
Maine	–	–	–	Utah	1	–	1
Maryland	6	–	6	Vermont	–	–	–
Massachusetts	–	–	–	Virginia	25	1	26
Michigan	–	1	1	Washington	1	1	2
Minnesota	3	–	3	West Virginia	12	1	13
Mississippi	217	68	285	Wisconsin	1	–	1
Missouri	40	1	41	Wyoming	8	1	9
Montana	8	1	9	TOTAL	1595	291	1886

OUNTIES IN THE UNITED STATES
1931
PARTMENT, TUSKEGEE INSTITUTE)

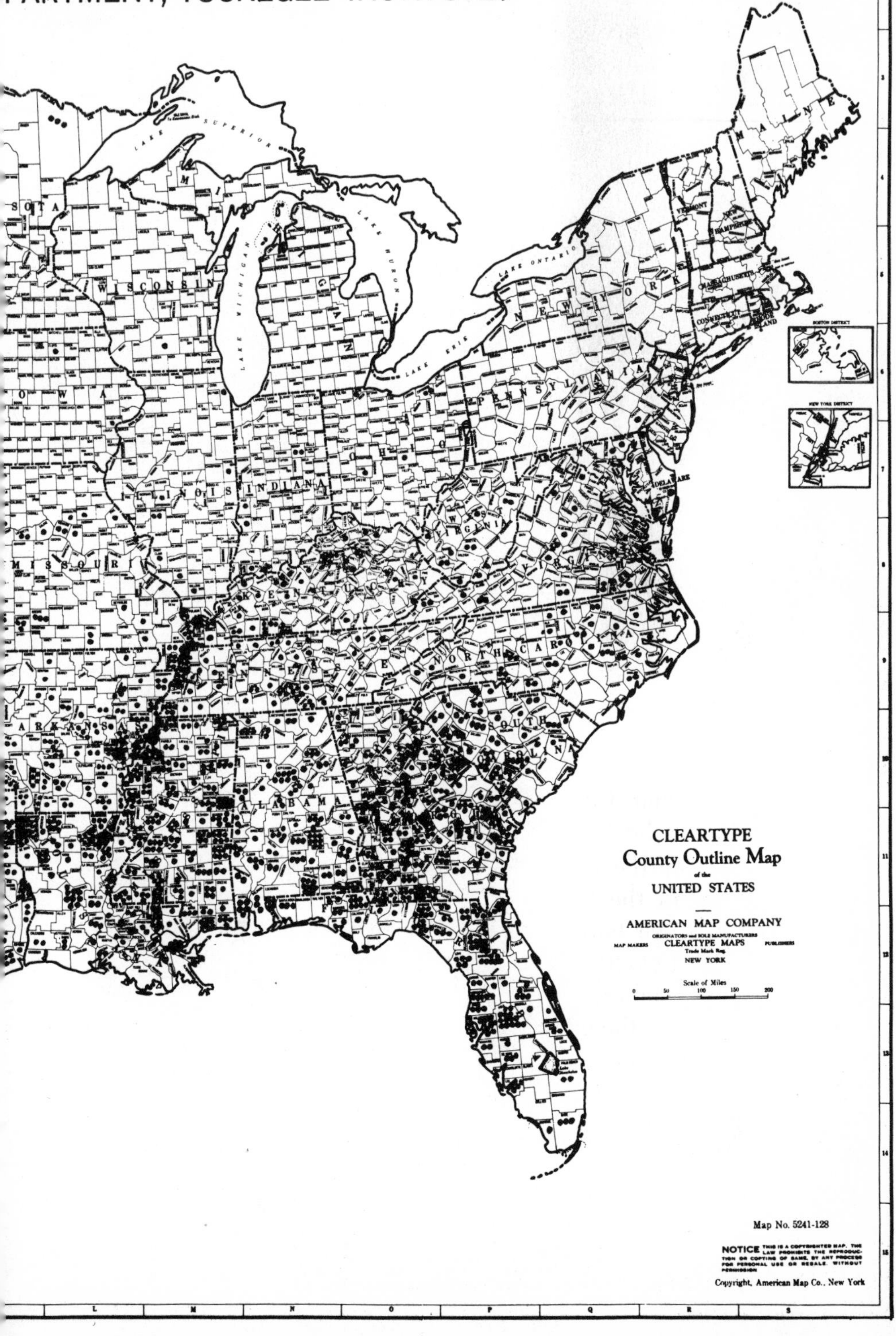

LAKE SUPERIOR
LAKE MICHIGAN
LAKE HURON
LAKE ONTARIO
LAKE ERIE
MAINE
VERMONT
NEW HAMPSHIRE
MASSACHUSETTS
CONNECTICUT
RHODE ISLAND
NEW YORK
PENNSYLVANIA
DELAWARE
MICHIGAN
WISCONSIN
MINNESOTA
IOWA
ILLINOIS
INDIANA
OHIO
WEST VIRGINIA
VIRGINIA
MISSOURI
KENTUCKY
TENNESSEE
NORTH CAROLINA
SOUTH CAROLINA
ARKANSAS
ALABAMA
BOSTON DISTRICT
NEW YORK DISTRICT
CLEARTYPE
County Outline Map
of the
UNITED STATES
AMERICAN MAP COMPANY
ORIGINATORS and SOLE MANUFACTURERS
MAP MAKERS
CLEARTYPE MAPS
PUBLISHERS
Trade Mark Reg.
NEW YORK
Scale of Miles
0 50 100 150 200
Map No. 5241-128
NOTICE THIS IS A COPYRIGHTED MAP. THE LAW PROHIBITS THE REPRODUCTION OR COPYING OF SAME, BY ANY PROCESS FOR PERSONAL USE OR RESALE, WITHOUT PERMISSION
Copyright, American Map Co., New York
L M N O P Q R S

Klan cross-burning

licensed to hate Catholics, Jews, the foreign-born—anyone who was not "one hundred per cent American." With this broadened hate program the Klan established dens in the North and West as well as in the South. In 1919 robed Klansmen paraded in more than two hundred American cities.

For the NAACP, "The Red Summer" started early and ended late. Staff members had hurried to riot-torn areas to dig out the facts and give them the widest possible publicity. Digging out the facts often called for the talents of a secret agent.

In the small town of Elaine, Arkansas, sharecroppers had formed a union in the hope of receiving a fairer settlement of

Walter White

their accounts. When whites fired into the church where they were meeting, the sharecroppers returned their fire. The death of a white man touched off a week-long massacre of Negroes. By the time it was over more than sixty black men and five whites were dead. Hundreds of "black revolutionists," as local papers called them, were arrested. In trials that lasted less than an hour, sixty-seven received long prison terms and twelve were sentenced to death. The only white man arrested was the lawyer for the sharecroppers' union.

Walter White, assistant secretary of the NAACP, was in Chicago collecting evidence against ringleaders of a riot there when newspapers reported the "black insurrection" in Elaine. Wearily he packed his bag and headed for Arkansas. Although he was a Negro he was so fair-skinned that he was easily mistaken for white. Posing as a reporter, he stopped first in Little Rock to interview the governor. "I am delighted that a northern newspaper has sent so able and experienced a reporter to answer the foul lies that infamous National Association for the Advancement of Colored People have been telling about the good people of Arkansas," the governor told him.

Armed with a letter of introduction from the governor, White then went to Helena where the sharecroppers were in jail. After talking to white witnesses of the "revolution" he asked to speak to the prisoners alone. He was walking down the street to the jail when a Negro overtook him.

"Mister, I've got something to tell you," the man whispered out of the corner of his mouth. "Follow me."

White followed. When they were hidden by a clump of trees at the edge of town, the man explained. "I heard them talking about you—the white folks. They say they are going to get you. I figured that if the white folks are so against you, you must be a friend of ours."

There were two trains a day out of Helena. White caught the first one with only seconds to spare. "You're leaving just when the fun is going to start," the conductor told him as the train pulled away from the station. "There's a damned yellow nigger down here passing for white and the boys are going to get him."

"What'll they do with him?" White asked in a voice that he hoped was steady.

The conductor shook his head. "When they get through with him he won't pass for white no more!"

Secret agent White passed for white again and again in order to investigate lynchings, but it was a long time before he returned to Arkansas. He reported that the Elaine riot was not an "uprising of Negroes but rather a pogrom* by whites" and

* The word "pogrom" comes from Czarist Russia where Russians conducted organized massacres—pogroms—of Jews.

that it stemmed from the "systematic robbery of Negro tenant farmers and sharecroppers." The facts he brought back aroused national concern for the condemned men.

Three times gallows were built to hang the sharecroppers of Elaine and three times NAACP lawyers managed to stay their execution. At last, in February 1923, the Supreme Court ruled that the men had not received a fair trial. The courtroom, said Chief Justice Holmes, had been "dominated by a mob" and "counsel, jury and judge were swept by an irresistible wave of public passion." The men were freed and the Court's decision became a weapon in the fight to protect accused persons, white as well as Negro, against "lynching by law."

"Lynching by law" made headlines again in the 1930s when nine Negro teen-agers, aged thirteen to nineteen, were arrested in Scottsboro, Alabama. Charged with attacking two white girls, they were convicted by an all-white jury and all but the thirteen-year-old were sentenced to death. As their story leaked out, sympathy for the boys became widespread. Articles, books and a Broadway play, *They Shall Not Die*, were written about them. In Europe, United States embassies were snowed under with petitions: "Free the Scottsboro Boys!"

Their case was appealed, retried, and twice taken to the Supreme Court. Teams of lawyers supplied at different times by the NAACP, the International Labor Defense and the Scottsboro Defense Committee finally succeeded in saving the boys' lives, although they served long jail terms.

The Supreme Court ruling in their case established the right of a Negro to be tried by a jury that did not exclude Negroes from its panel. This was a right guaranteed by the Fourteenth Amendment and by a law passed by Congress in 1875, but since the end of reconstruction the law had not been enforced.

While fighting "lynching by law" the NAACP continued to campaign against lynching by mob. Moorfield Storey, the Association's president and a distinguished Boston lawyer, drew up a bill that made lynching a federal offense and allowed the Justice Department to take action against lynchers if local sheriffs failed to do so. Congressman L. C. Dyer of Missouri introduced the bill into Congress in 1919. To win support for it, the NAACP ran full-page advertisements in newspapers:

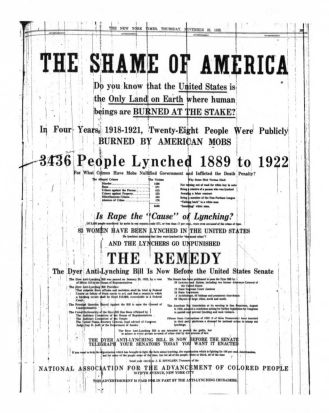

During the next years James Weldon Johnson spent most of his time in Washington buttonholing congressmen to convince them of the need for the bill. The Dyer Bill was passed by the House in 1922 but it died in the Senate. By that time the Klan boasted a membership of two million, including at least one senator, and politicians had a wholesome respect for the Invisible Empire.

As Klan power weakened in the '30s, the fight against lynching received wider support. In the South, white churchwomen formed the Association of Southern Women for the Prevention of Lynching. In the North, writers joined the Writers League Against Lynching and artists contributed paintings and sculpture for an "Art Commentary." Audiences were shaken when blues singer Billie Holliday sang "Strange Fruit":

Southern trees bear a strange fruit,
Blood on the leaves and blood at the root;

Black body swinging in the Southern breeze,
Strange fruit hanging from the poplar trees

Pastoral scene of the gallant South
The bulging eyes and the twisted mouth;

Scent of magnolia sweet and fresh
And the sudden smell of burning flesh

Here is a fruit for the crows to pluck,
For the rain to gather, for the wind to suck,
For the sun to rot, for the tree to drop,
Here is a strange and bitter crop.

"Strange Fruit" became a part of the language, and the title of a best-selling novel by Lillian Smith of Georgia, but it did not convince Congress to take action. Walter White, who succeeded James Weldon Johnson as NAACP executive secretary, saw one hundred and thirty separate antilynching bills offered in Congress between 1934 and 1940. Some died in committee. Some were approved in the House only to be blocked in the Senate, whose rules permitted a handful of southerners to talk them to death.

Under the pressure of public opinion, the number of lynchings declined. Mobs no longer burned human beings at the stake, but southern white men continued to bomb, beat and gun down those whom they disliked and southern juries remained unwilling to convict them for their crimes. After almost half a century, the NAACP and other civil rights groups are still fighting for a law that will make racial violence a federal crime, as kidnaping is, and that will permit the government to prosecute the murderers of Negroes and white civil rights workers.

Castles and Men

In 1925 the Association was called on to defend an old English law that said, "A man's home is his castle." The man in question was Dr. Ossian Sweet, a surgeon who had been living with his in-laws in a crowded apartment in Detroit. His "castle" was a two-story brick house at the corner of Garland and Charlevoix streets, some blocks from the black ghetto.

As soon as Dr. Sweet made a down payment on the house he began to receive threatening letters: "No niggers wanted . . . You had better not show your damned black face here." Mrs. Sweet, who had grown up in a mixed neighborhood in Detroit, put them down as crank letters. Dr. Sweet, a native of Florida, was less sure. All that summer, the Klan held meetings in the city while a neighborhood "improvement association" announced that it would fight to keep out "undesirables." As the days grew cooler, the Sweets arranged to move to their new home.

The police were notified, the baby left with Mrs. Sweet's parents, and on the morning of September 8 two small vans headed for Garland Street. Dr. Sweet's brothers and some friends joined them as moving men unloaded the furniture. Along with tables, chairs and bedding, the men carried in a supply of food and a case that contained ten guns and almost four hundred rounds of ammunition. The man in the castle was prepared for a siege.

Their first night was quiet but on the second hundreds of people gathered on the street outside the house. Mrs. Sweet was in the kitchen cooking dinner when a stone crashed through a window. All over the house shades were drawn. Now Dr. Sweet switched off the lights.

Lynching victims

"Niggers! Niggers! Get the niggers!" the crowd screamed. Bricks followed stones. Above the sound of breaking glass, shots could be heard. From an upstairs window, the defenders of the castle returned the fire. One of the attackers fell dead.

Suddenly the police, who had ignored the crowd a short time earlier, arrived in full force. Entering the house they arrested all its occupants, ten men and Mrs. Sweet, and hustled them to jail. The charge was murder in the first degree.

Negroes from Maine to Mississippi sent a flood of dimes and dollars for the Sweets' defense. The NAACP was able to persuade Clarence Darrow, the country's best-known lawyer, to represent them. They had another stroke of luck. The judge assigned to the trial was Frank Murphy, a courageous liberal who later became a Supreme Court Justice.

Basing his case on a man's right to defend his home, Darrow turned the court into a classroom for the teaching of Negro history. The secretary of Detroit's Urban League testified about the lack of housing in the ghetto. Dr. Sweet told of race riots he had seen in Washington and elsewhere. Reviewing the whole ugly story of anti-Negro violence, he described his feelings on the night of the shooting.

"I realized I was facing the same mob that had hounded my people through its entire history. I had my back against the wall. I knew what mobs had done before."

When white witnesses claimed that the crowd on Garland Street had been neighborly, Darrow mocked them. "Neighbors!" he snorted. "Neighbors in the sense an undertaker is when he comes to carry out a corpse. They had gathered as the Roman populace gathered at the Coliseum to see the slaves fed to the lions. I want to be fair. Are the people of this neighborhood worse than other people? I don't think they are. These people honestly believe colored people are an inferior race. I don't. They are obsessed with fanaticism. And when people are obsessed they become cruel.

"But, gentlemen"—he faced the jury—"they oughtn't to ask you to be cruel for them. There is nothing but prejudice in this case. If it was reversed and eleven white men had shot and killed a black while protecting their home no one would have dreamed of having them indicted. They would have been given medals instead."

After deliberating for three hours, the jury returned with a verdict of not guilty.*

---

* The case was won but Mrs. Sweet caught a bad cold during her stay in the drafty Wayne County jail. The cold and the strain of the trial so weakened her that she developed tuberculosis and died.

"HOW CAN WE FIGHT FOR DEMOCRACY
IN BURMA WHEN WE DON'T HAVE
DEMOCRACY IN BIRMINGHAM?"

A. *Philip Randolph, 1942*

CHAPTER 13

New Deal

Depression!

DON'T BUY WHERE YOU CAN'T WORK. Men and women walked along the street holding signs. "Don't buy, brother," they chanted. "Stay out of that store until the man gives you a job."

The year was 1932, the worst year of the Great Depression. Factories were closed and people were jobless, hungry, frightened. Negroes were the hardest hit of all. One out of every two black Americans was unemployed. Even in the ghettos, the jobs were held by whites. The clerks in grocery stores, the cashiers in movie theaters, the waiters in restaurants were white. So were milkmen, insurance collectors, the men who read the electric meters, the bus and truck drivers.

In St. Louis, members of the Urban League boycotted a store until it took on some Negro employees. Soon a Jobs-for-Negroes campaign spread to all the big cities in the North. Committees of ghetto dwellers called on local merchants to ask them to hire Negroes. If they refused, pickets appeared in front of their stores with signs saying, DON'T BUY WHERE YOU CAN'T WORK.

In Pittsburgh, the Negro Housewives League stopped buying milk until the local dairy hired Negro drivers. In Harlem, a young minister named Adam Clayton Powell led parades to the offices of the electric company. At the cashier's window, the paraders solemnly handed over bags filled with pennies. They were paying their electric bills—and tying up the bookkeeping department for days. Powell also organized black-out nights when Harlem residents used candles instead of electricity, and telephone hours when the phone company switchboards were flooded with calls to "Operator."

As a result of these protests, the ghetto stores and the big utility companies slowly changed their hiring policies. Negroes became sales clerks, meter readers, telephone operators, repairmen. Even city bus companies gave in and hired some black drivers and mechanics. Thousands of Negroes won jobs—but millions were still left without work.

When Franklin D. Roosevelt was elected President he promised a "New Deal." Relief programs were started to make sure that no one starved, and the government spent billions of dollars to build schools, housing projects, playgrounds, roads. Negroes got a share, although often not a fair share, of the jobs.

They also took part in the new trade union movement that grew out of the Depression. The Committee for Industrial Organization, known as the CIO, was founded in 1935. The CIO organized workers along industrial rather than craft lines. Instead of a separate union for painters, another for carpenters, all of the workers in the same factory joined the same union. Although Negroes were still shut out of most AF of L unions, they were accepted in the CIO. Together with white workers, they won union contracts in the steel, auto and other big industries.

During the Depression, the exodus from the South continued. As more and more Negroes voted in northern cities they began to win some representation in local and state governments. Chicago's South Side, which had the greatest concentration of black voters, sent a Negro to Congress in 1928. Oscar De Priest, the first black man in the House since George White, was succeeded by Arthur Mitchell and Mitchell by William L. Dawson, the present Negro congressman from Chicago. New

*Congressman Adam Clayton Powell (right) with New York's Mayor
La Guardia*

York's black voters sent Adam Clayton Powell to the City
Council in 1941 and to Congress in 1944.

The Washington to which Powell came had changed since
Wilson's day. During the New Deal, Roosevelt appointed Negro
economists, lawyers, educators to a number of federal agencies.
Ralph Bunche had a post in the State Department, Robert C.
Weaver in the Department of the Interior and Mrs. Mary
McLeod Bethune was Director of Negro Affairs for the National Youth Administration. Along with these prominent men
and women, who were called Roosevelt's "Black Cabinet," the
number of Negroes in civil service jobs doubled, then quad-
rupled during the New Deal.

Washington had changed, yet in many ways it was the same. There was still segregation in some government offices and outside of government offices there was segregation everywhere. No downtown hotel would rent a room to a Negro. No downtown restaurant would serve him. No downtown theater would admit him even to the balcony. Hazel Scott, Powell's wife, had a starring role in the film *Rhapsody in Blue*. When it played in Washington the Powells could not see it.

On Capitol Hill an unwritten law kept Negro congressmen from the House dining room, gymnasium and barbershop. The representatives from Chicago had observed this "law" but Adam Clayton Powell refused to obey it. He used all of the congressional facilities and insisted that his staff do the same. "When I heard that the dining room for representatives' staff was off limits to Negroes," he said, "I told my secretary and clerks to go down there and eat whether they were hungry or not."

Good Will

The Negro who made the greatest impact on white America during the Depression was neither a congressman nor a "Black Cabinet" member. She was a shy woman, uninterested in politics, who happened to have one of the finest singing voices in the world. Marian Anderson was scheduled to give a concert in Washington. But the Daughters of the American Revolution who own Constitution Hall, the city's only suitable auditorium, refused to allow a Negro to sing there.

Eleanor Roosevelt, the President's wife, promptly resigned from the DAR. Leading musicians sent telegrams cancelling their own appearances at the hall. Though Marian Anderson had no comment for the press, the NAACP and two dozen other national and local organizations formed a Marian Anderson Protest Committee. With a list of sponsors that read like

Marian Anderson

Marian Anderson sings at Lincoln Memorial

a Who's Who of the capital, the committee arranged to have Miss Anderson give an outdoor concert in Washington that would be open to all comers.

On Easter Sunday in 1939, tall brown-skinned Marian Anderson walked up the steps of the Lincoln Memorial. Supreme Court justices, senators, congressmen, Cabinet members sat on the platform, ringing the marble statue of Lincoln. Below, as far as she could see, were people—row after row after row, from the Memorial grounds to the foot of the Washington Monument, blocks away.

"I had a feeling that a great wave of good will poured out from these people, almost engulfing me," she said. "When I stood up to sing our national anthem I felt for a moment as though I were choking. For a desperate second I thought that the words would not come."

The words came. She sang. For an hour, hatred and prejudice were stilled as the nation listened to Marian Anderson, moved by the beauty of her music, by her grace and dignity.

For years afterward, people came up to her to say, "You know, I was at that Easter concert." When a mural commemorating the occasion was painted in the Department of the Interior building, Secretary of the Interior Harold Ickes said, "Her voice and personality have come to be a symbol of the immortal truth that 'all men are created free and equal.'"

The wave of good will that Marian Anderson felt was real. The harsh years of the Depression had put everyone in the same boat for a time. When Franklin D. Roosevelt talked on the radio of "the forgotten man" or the third of a nation that was "ill-housed, ill-clad, ill-nourished," people realized, with a surge of conscience, that he was speaking of blacks as well as whites.

In the South, interracial groups were started. The Southern Conference for Human Welfare held its founding convention in Birmingham, Alabama, in 1938. When the delegates met in the Municipal Auditorium, police surrounded the building to make sure that the segregation laws were obeyed. Negro delegates were forced to sit on one side of the aisle, whites on the other. Mrs. Roosevelt, one of the principal speakers, placed her chair squarely in the middle.

The Southern Conference worked to end segregation in housing, voting, transportation—and in municipal auditoriums. The latter was not an easy task. Each year the Conference gave a

Thomas Jefferson Award to the Southerner who had given "the most outstanding service in the field of human welfare in line with the philosophy of Thomas Jefferson." The 1942 award went to Mrs. Mary McLeod Bethune. The auditorium in which she received it was not segregated, but she had to walk up six flights of stairs when she refused to ride in the freight elevator.

The Southern Conference, which later became the Southern Conference Educational Fund (SCEF), was followed by the Southern Regional Council. Also a joint effort of Negro and white Southerners "to attain equal opportunity for all peoples in the South," the Council believed that the "problems associated with two races living side by side can be solved . . . if they are brought out into an atmosphere of justice and good will."

The March That Never Was

After the outbreak of World War II in Europe, President Roosevelt called on the United States to become "the arsenal of democracy." Financed by government contracts, factories began to turn out planes, ships, tanks, guns. The Depression was over.

But not for Negroes.

While France fell to Hitler's armies, a U.S. defense plant in Kansas advertised for "White American citizens" only. While Nazi planes rained bombs on England, the head of an aircraft company in California declared, "It is against company policy to employ Negroes as aircraft workers and mechanics." However, he added, "there will be some jobs as janitors."

The United States Employment Service reported, early in 1941, that out of eight thousand new workers in aviation plants, only thirteen were Negroes. Electrical equipment plants had hired a thousand new workers, five of them Negro. Thirty-five thousand men had found work in machine and tool shops; two hundred and forty-five were Negroes. Negroes were not only denied skilled jobs in war plants, the report said, "but are receiving very few jobs of any type."

Negroes did not need to read the report. In spite of the hopes raised by the New Deal, they saw the same old one. Good will, heartwarming as it was to people who had felt so little of it, didn't buy groceries or pay the rent. They had learned something, however, from the Jobs-for-Negroes campaign and the CIO organizing drive. Asa Philip Randolph, president of the Brotherhood of Sleeping Car Porters, proposed a March on Washington to demand jobs in defense industries.

"The administration leaders will never give the Negro justice," Randolph said, "until they see ten, twenty, fifty thousand Negroes on the White House lawn."

A March-on-Washington committee was set up with headquarters in Harlem and branch offices in other cities. Supported by the NAACP, the Urban League, the National Council of Negro Women and dozens of churches and clubs, the committee made plans for a pilgrimage to the capital on July 1, 1941. Buses and trains were chartered and thousands of people began to save up money for fares.

In May, Randolph sent out a "Call to Negro America." We have "power, great power," he said. "Our problem is to hitch it up for action on the broadest, most daring and most gigantic scale. An all-out thundering March will gain respect for the Negro people. It will create a new sense of self-respect among Negroes.

"We shall not call upon our white friends to march with us," he added. "There are some things Negroes must do alone. Negroes should supply the money, make the sacrifices, and endure the suffering to break down the barriers to full citizenship rights in America."

Until Randolph's "Call," newspapers—except for the Negro press—had ignored the March. Now official Washington was alarmed. A large-scale protest against American racism at a time when our allies were fighting Nazi racism was at the very least embarrassing. Early in June Mrs. Roosevelt made a trip

A. Philip Randolph

to New York to ask the March committee to call off the demonstration. After her mission failed, the President sent for A. Philip Randolph and Walter White.

When the two men entered the White House they found the Secretary of the Navy, the Assistant Secretary of War, and the president of General Motors waiting for them in Roosevelt's office. Randolph and White recited the facts of discrimination.

"How many people will *really* march?" Roosevelt interrupted.

"Not less than one hundred thousand," White answered.

For a long moment, the President looked at him as if to see if he were bluffing. Then he asked, "What do you want me to do?"

"Issue an executive order abolishing discrimination in all government departments and national defense jobs," Randolph replied.

That afternoon A. Philip Randolph and Walter White sat in the Cabinet Room of the White House drawing up the kind of order they wanted. For an anxious week, their draft was rewritten, whittled down, strengthened again. On June 25, 1941 —six days before the March was to take place—President Roosevelt issued Executive Order 8802: ". . . There shall be no discrimination in the employment of workers in defense industries or government because of race, creed, color, or national origin . . . It is the duty of employers and of labor organizations . . . to provide for the full and equitable participation of all workers in defense industries, without discrimination . . ."

The order set up a Fair Employment Practices Committee "to investigate complaints of discrimination" and to "take appropriate steps to redress grievances." During the five years of its existence the FEPC opened up tens of thousands of jobs for Negroes. Lacking enforcement powers, it failed to wipe out discrimination. But it was a step toward equal opportunity in employment, and it was followed by others.

Speaking on a nationwide radio hookup, Randolph "postponed" the March. At victory celebrations on July 1, the

President's order was hailed as a "Second Emancipation Procla-mation." The March-That-Never-Was showed Negroes that they had power when they hitched up for action. "We get more when we yell than we do when we plead," observed Roy Wilkins of the NAACP.

The Right to Fight

On the morning of December 7, 1941, a general alarm sounded on the U.S.S. *Arizona,* which was riding at anchor at Pearl Harbor. Dorie Miller, messman third class, left his station in the galley and ran on the double to the deck. Low-flying planes were strafing the ship. On the bridge, the *Arizona's* captain lay dying. After helping to move him to shelter, Miller took a machine gun from the hands of a dead gunner. By the time the order came to abandon ship, he had brought down four Japanese planes. When he was awarded a Navy Cross for "extreme courage," his citation said, "Without previ-ous experience, he manned a machine gun in the face of serious fire, shooting down four enemy planes."

Without previous experience! Dorie Miller, one of the first American heroes of World War II, had no experience as a gunner because he was black. Negroes, said the Navy, may not rise above the rank of messmen (kitchen helpers). Negroes, said the Army, must train and fight in separate regiments. Negroes, said the Marine and Air Corps, cannot be accepted at all.

Dorie Miller went down to his death with the *Liscombe Bay* two years later, still a messman. But his heroism, and a barrage of protests from other Negroes, brought about some changes. The Navy began to train Negroes as gunners, radio-men, ship's carpenters, although they were limited to shore duty until 1944. The Army desegregated its officers' training camps and promoted Colonel Benjamin O. Davis, Sr., highest ranking

Dorie Miller receives the Navy Cross

Negro officer, to brigadier general. The Marine Corps broke with its 167-year-old tradition to accept Negro volunteers. The day after a Howard University student sued to compel the War Department to train him as a pilot, the Air Force set up a school for Negro airmen at Tuskegee Institute.

More than a million black Americans were in uniform before the end of the war, but the armed forces were still Jim Crow. Even Negroes who were trained for combat were used for pick-and-shovel work. Army post exchanges and recreation centers remained separate and unequal. Negro soldiers who ventured into southern towns when off duty were often beaten and sometimes killed by local police. German prisoners of war were served meals in railway dining cars, while the Negro soldiers who guarded them went hungry. In a poem titled DEFEAT, Witter Bynner described one of these incidents:

> *On a train in Texas German prisoners eat*
> *With white American soldiers, seat by seat*
> *While black American soldiers sit apart—*
> *The white men eating meat, the black men heart.*

Negroes "ate heart" too, when the Red Cross started blood banks to collect and store blood for men wounded in battle. Along with other patriotic citizens, they offered to give blood. At first they were turned away. Later blood from Negro donors was accepted but was separated from "white" blood. Although the American Medical Association and leading scientists insisted that there was no possible difference between the blood of Negroes and whites, the Red Cross, backed by the Army, continued to label the cartons of blood plasma NEGRO and WHITE. Segregation of blood was doubly painful because the man who made blood banks a practical reality was a Negro. Dr. Charles R. Drew had written a thesis on "Banked Blood" while studying for a graduate degree at Columbia University. His thesis became the blueprint for early blood storage projects in England and the United States. In 1941 he served as director of the Red Cross's first blood bank.

Dr. Charles R. Drew

Every Negro knew about Dr. Drew, and every Negro knew the tragic end of his story.

After the war he was driving from Washington with three other doctors to attend a medical conference at a southern college. In North Carolina their car skidded and rolled over. Dr. Drew was badly hurt. He was losing blood rapidly when a passing car took him to the nearest hospital. At its emergency entrance, hospital attendants waved him away.

"Take him to the colored hospital," they said. "We don't treat Negroes here."

His companions took him to the colored hospital. On the way, Dr. Charles Drew bled to death.*

Negro resentments mounted during the war. "White folks talking about the Four Freedoms," a man grumbled, "and we ain't got any." "That Hitler!" a girl wrote in a school composition. "I'd like to paint him black and send him to Georgia." "No injustice embitters Negroes more than continued segregation and discrimination in the armed forces," said a statement issued by twenty-five Negro organizations.

Sometimes the bitterness boiled over. Negroes in Harlem rioted after a policeman shot a Negro soldier. There was a hunger strike at a Seabee camp in California, "mutinies" in San Francisco and Hawaii and a near-insurrection on Guam. The NAACP was besieged with mail from servicemen, asking for help. Wearing a war correspondent's uniform, Walter White traveled to Europe and the Pacific to investigate complaints.

"For what were you court-martialed the first time?" he asked a prisoner on Guam.

"I sat down in a bus on a seat that wasn't for colored."

"What happened then?"

"They arrested me and put me in solitary confinement for five days on bread and water."

"And what was the charge the second time?"

---

* Dr. Drew was not the only Negro to lose his life because a hospital refused him first aid. Bessie Smith, the great blues singer, died under similar circumstances after an auto accident in Mississippi in 1937.

"I went into a white restaurant and asked to be served food."

"What happened then?"

"The same sentence, sir. Solitary confinement on bread and water for five days."

Everywhere White went, soldiers and sailors told him, "Our battle for democracy will begin when we reach home!"

After the war, A. Philip Randolph formed the Committee Against Jim Crow in Military Service and Training. At a Senate hearing he warned that Negroes would refuse to serve when drafted unless conditions improved. By this time many Americans realized that segregated military training was wasteful as well as wrong. In the summer of 1948 President Truman issued an executive order calling for "Equality of treatment and opportunity for all persons in the armed services without regard to race, color, religion or national origin."

Time and the Korean War ended segregation in the Army and Navy. All-Negro units were abolished. Recreation centers were integrated. In the 1960s military commanders were told to oppose discrimination not only on army bases but in nearby communities where soldiers' families lived.

"We have come a long way since President Truman ordered the desegregation of the Armed Forces," President Kennedy wrote in 1963. "Yet a great deal remains to be done."

A great deal still remains to be done. More than seventeen thousand men and women serve on local draft boards across the country, but in January 1968 only 3.8 per cent were Negro. Draft boards in Alabama and Mississippi have no Negro members, in spite of the large number of Negroes living in both states.

The only Negro general officer on active duty in all the services is Lieutenant General Benjamin O. Davis, Jr., whose father was the first Negro general in the army. "We're all getting a little worried," Whitney Young of the Urban League wryly observed, "because General Davis, Jr. hasn't had a son."

White and Negro soldiers in Vietnam

Nonetheless, the military is far ahead of industry in offering Negro youth skilled jobs and equal pay. "The Army is taking care of me and my family," said a paratrooper at Fort Bragg. "There's no job in South Carolina that would pay me as much." "I like the service," said a sergeant. "And anyway, the alternative is to go back to Birmingham." "Can I go back to New Orleans —or anywhere else—and get a job as an aircraft mechanic?" asked another enlisted man. "I don't think so."

Because the rest of American society has failed to provide equal opportunities, proportionately more Negroes are serving in today's army than whites. More are being drafted. More are volunteering. More are signing up for combat units like the paratroopers which offer extra pay. And more are dying in battle. Although Negroes make up only 11 per cent of the population of the United States, 22 per cent of the men killed in action in Vietnam recently are black.

"AFTER MORE THAN TWO HUNDRED YEARS IN
SLAVERY AND NINETY OF QUASI-FREEDOM, IT
IS HARD TO THINK VERY HIGHLY OF WILLIAM
FAULKNER'S ADVICE TO 'GO SLOW.' 'THEY
DON'T MEAN GO SLOW,' THURGOOD MARSHALL IS
REPORTED TO HAVE SAID, 'THEY MEAN DON'T GO.'"

James Baldwin

CHAPTER 14

The Law Department

The Right to a Home

During the Depression years, the NAACP hired its first full-time lawyer and made plans for a long-range legal battle against discrimination. In the North, its Legal Committee turned its attention to the devices that kept Negroes in ghettos.

In 1938, Carl Hansberry, a well-to-do Chicagoan, bought a home in a "white" neighborhood. His neighbors-to-be tried to evict him because the house was covered by a restrictive covenant that forbade its sale to a black man. After the state courts ruled against him, Carl Hansberry and NAACP attorneys took his case to the Supreme Court.

His eight-year-old daughter, Lorraine, never forgot the howling, stone-throwing mobs that collected in front of their house or her mother's nightly patrol with a loaded pistol while her father was in Washington. Until neighbors threw stones at his children, Carl Hansberry had been optimistic about the future of American Negroes. Although the Supreme Court decided in his favor, his neighbors' hatred drove him from the United States. He bought a home in Mexico but before he could move his family there he died—"of a cerebral hemorrhage, supposedly," his daughter said, "but American racism helped kill him."

Years later, Lorraine Hansberry wrote *A Raisin in the Sun*, an award-winning play that was made into a film. In it she told of the hopes and dreams of a Negro family who tried to escape from Chicago's black ghetto.

The decision in the Hansberry case outlawed restrictive covenants only in one area in Chicago. When Mr. and Mrs. J. D. Shelley bought a home in St. Louis at the end of World War II they, too, ran up against a restrictive covenant. Thirty years earlier the owner of their house had signed an agreement not to sell to "people of the Negro or Mongolian Race." By the time the case of Shelley *vs.* Kraemer reached the Supreme Court, the NAACP had the backing of a number of national and international organizations as well as the federal government. Three of the Supreme Court justices disqualified themselves when they found, to their embarrassment, that the deeds to their own homes contained racial restrictions. In May 1948, the remaining six justices ruled that restrictive covenants could not be enforced, because they denied "equality in the enjoyment of property rights" and thus violated the Fourteenth Amendment.

The decision was an important one, affecting not only Negroes but Jews, Chinese and other minority groups that had been barred from exclusive neighborhoods. The Court had knocked down the legal props that held up the ghetto walls but it had no power to prevent unwritten gentleman's agreements— or mobs.

In 1951 Harvey Clark, a young Negro war veteran, rented an apartment in Cicero, a suburb of Chicago. When he moved in with his family, five thousand men and women stormed the building. While police watched, water and gas were turned on, windows smashed, fires set. Tossing the Clarks' belongings into the street, the mob built a bonfire with their beds, chairs and a piano bought for their daughter Michele's music lessons.

After the National Guard restored order a grand jury indicted the Clarks and their NAACP lawyer for starting a riot!

Although the indictments were dismissed and sympathetic people from all over the country contributed money to buy a new piano for Michele, the Clarks were forced to move to an all-black neighborhood in Chicago. Today fifteen thousand Negroes work in Cicero's factories and restaurants, but Cicero is still lily-white.

The Right to Vote

A favorite story told by Negroes in the South concerned a man who was bound and determined to vote. He had studied the state and federal constitutions until he knew them backward and forward. Confident that he could answer all questions, he went to the election board and asked to register. For an hour, the registrar quizzed him. Her questions became harder and harder, but she wasn't able to trip him. After he had explained every clause in the constitutions she left the room to consult with other board members. She returned with a pleased smile on her face.

"John," she said, "can you tell me the meaning of the phrase *habeas corpus ad testificandum?*"

"I expect I can." John nodded and reached for his hat. "It means Negroes aren't gonna be allowed to vote around here nohow."

For more than fifty years, southern Negroes weren't allowed to vote "nohow." After reconstruction when Negro voting stopped, the Republican Party lost most of its strength in the South. Almost all voters were Democrats. As a result, the "real" elections took place in the Democratic primaries because it was there that candidates for state and local offices were chosen.

The NAACP fought a long uphill fight for the right of

Negroes to vote in the primaries. As far back as 1927, Dr. L. A. Nixon of El Paso challenged a Texas law that said, "In no event shall a Negro be eligible to participate in a Democratic primary election." When the Supreme Court agreed that the law was unconstitutional, Texans shrugged their shoulders and passed another law. The new one authorized "every political party through its State Executive Committee to prescribe the qualifications of its own members." The Democratic State Executive Committee had little trouble deciding that its members must be white.

Again Dr. Nixon sued. Again the NAACP lawyers won his case. Again Texans shrugged their shoulders. This time a Democratic convention rather than the executive committee voted for an all-white membership and the Supreme Court upheld them.

The matter rested there until 1940 when Dr. Lonnie Smith tried to vote in a primary in Houston. "Boy, get the hell away from here," he was told. "Who ever heard of a Negro voting?"

The NAACP had. Thurgood Marshall, head of the Association's new Legal Defense and Educational Fund, went with Dr. Smith to the Supreme Court. In 1944 the Court ruled that "the right to vote in a primary is a right secured by the Constitution."

Before the NAACP had a chance to celebrate its victory, other southern states searched for loopholes. Two weeks after the Court's decision, the governor of South Carolina called his legislature into special session. Asking them to repeal all of the state's primary laws, he said, "White supremacy will be maintained in our primaries. Let the chips fall where they may!"

South Carolina's legislators repealed more than one hundred and fifty laws. As far as the state was concerned, the Democratic Party had become a private club. When George Elmore and other Negroes tried to vote in a 1946 primary, they were turned away.

Briefcase in hand, Thurgood Marshall soon appeared in Columbia, the state capital. He argued Elmore's case before Federal Judge J. Waties Waring. Waring was a South Carolina gentleman and a Democrat of long standing but he had been reading the United States Constitution. "For too many years the people of this country and particularly of this state have evaded realistic issues," he declared. "It is time for South Carolina to rejoin the Union. It is time to adopt the American way of conducting elections. All citizens are entitled to cast a ballot, and if the only realistic elections are clothed with the name primary, they are entitled to vote there."

While the rest of the South watched, South Carolina made one more try. In 1948 its Democratic Party adopted new rules. Certainly a Negro could vote in the primary—if he took an oath swearing to support the "social, religious and educational separation of races" and to oppose the Fair Employment Practices Committee. When David Brown refused to take this "white supremacy oath" his case also came before Judge Waring. Calling the new rules "a deliberate attempt to evade" his earlier decision, Waring ordered Democratic leaders to open their enrollment books to Negroes or go to jail. They obeyed.

The end of white primaries meant the slow beginning of Negro voting. In 1940 only 5 per cent of southern Negroes of voting age were registered. By 1960 Negro registration in the South had risen to 28 per cent. But the "understanding clause" and threats of violence still kept the majority from the polls.

Separate but Unequal

In the 1930s southern states spent three times as much on white pupils as on Negroes. The differences were even greater in country towns where Negro schools were often unpainted

The Negro School at Perry, Georgia

sheds, lacking blackboards, books and playground equipment. A government survey in 1933 found that in 532 schools for black children, 515 had outside toilets and 11 had no toilets at all.

The NAACP hacked away at these inequalities, although it was like cutting a path through a jungle with a penknife. In 1937, William Gibbs, a school principal in Montgomery County, Maryland, complained that white principals were paid more than twice as much as he. Even the white janitors in white schools received more than the teachers in Negro schools. The differences in pay were so shocking that a Maryland court ordered the board of education to equalize them. But this was only one county and one board of education. The fight for equal pay for teachers had to be carried on in county after county, state after state.

In a fifteen-year period, the NAACP won fifty teachers' pay cases. That still left wide areas of the South where Negro teachers were underpaid.

Another glaring example of inequality was in higher education. Southern states made no provision for law schools, medical schools, schools of journalism for Negroes. Lloyd Gaines, a Missouri black man, wanted to become a lawyer. Since there was no law school for Negroes in his state he applied to the University of Missouri. When he was refused admission, the NAACP took his case to the Supreme Court. In 1938, the Court ordered Missouri to provide Gaines with an "equal" legal education.

After the Gaines decision, several southern states started graduate schools for Negroes. Others offered scholarships to northern schools. And every state began to pour money into Negro elementary and high schools on the theory that you never could tell where trouble would start next.

Trouble was certainly starting. Increasing numbers of Negro students were dissatisfied with makeshift graduate schools and were unwilling to go out-of-state for their education. Ada Sipuel refused to attend the separate law school that Oklahoma had taken two weeks to set up. After four years of court battles she became the first Negro admitted to the University of Oklahoma law school. Heman Sweatt refused to attend the separate law school that Texas set up for him. After four years of court battles he became the first Negro admitted to the University of Texas law school.

George McLaurin won admission to the University of Oklahoma's graduate school of education, but on a segregated basis. Like Frederick Douglass' daughter almost a century earlier, he was forced to sit in an anteroom outside of the classroom. In the library he was assigned a desk on the balcony. In the cafeteria he was given a special table. As soon as he appealed to the Supreme Court, the university's rules changed. McLaurin was allowed in the classroom, behind a railing marked RESERVED FOR COLORED. In 1950 the Court ruled that Oklahoma could not set McLaurin apart from other students. Said Chief Justice Vinson, he "must receive the same treatment at the hands of the state as students of other races." Not "separate and equal" but "the same!"

The Ghost of Homer Plessy

The biggest trouble of all was starting in Clarendon County
in rural South Carolina. When Reverend Joseph DeLaine called
a parents' meeting to talk about the schools for black children,
feelings boiled over. Angrily they counted up the "Nos." No
library. No gymnasium. No lunchroom. No auditorium. No
janitor to clean the rooms or stoke the stoves. At Ramby
Elementary School, no desks or electric lights.

The "white" schools had all these things and more. As
Negro children trudged along the road in the morning, the
white children rode by in a school bus. Sometimes shouts
came from the bus windows—"Niggers gotta walk!"

Perhaps this taunt hurt the most. When the Parent Committee
on Action was formed in 1947, the first request was for a
school bus. After the board of education waved them away,
the parents went to the NAACP. Their demand for a bus grew
into a suit for "Equal Educational Opportunities for Negro
Children."

While Reverend DeLaine collected the signatures of the
twenty parents who were bringing the suit, the NAACP called
a conference of lawyers in New York. For years they had
chipped away at the doctrine of "separate but equal." They
had won equal treatment for some teachers and graduate
students, but they had never challenged the "separate" part
of the rule. After the Supreme Court decisions in the Sweatt
and McLaurin cases, didn't it seem as if the ghost of Homer
Plessy was stirring?

The conference of lawyers was followed by conferences with
psychologists, sociologists, historians, educators. When the
Clarendon County case was heard in Charleston, South Carolina, in May 1951, the NAACP had changed direction. The
time had come, said Thurgood Marshall, "to go for the whole
hog. We decided to make segregation itself our target."

Marshall opened his case in a courtroom packed with people.
Negroes in Sunday-best clothes came from all over the state,

newspapermen from all over the country. There was a feeling that history was in the making.

Clarendon's school officials readily agreed that the schools for colored children were poor. They brought in blueprints and builders' estimates to show that they were planning to build new, better schools. Marshall answered them by calling psychologists and other social scientists to the witness stand. His experts testified that new buildings would not solve the problem. The separation of Negroes from white children made them feel inferior and unwanted, and affected their personalities throughout their lives. The only way to give all children a truly equal education, Marshall summed up, was to end school segregation.

Two of the federal judges who heard the case rejected Marshall's experts, but the third, Judge J. W. Waring, had also seen the ghost of Homer Plessy. In a dissenting opinion, he said that "separate but equal" violated the constitutional rights of Negro children. "Segregation in education must go and must go now," he wrote. "Segregation is *per se* [of itself] inequality."

In Kansas, Virginia, Delaware and Washington, D.C., other Negro parents brought similar suits and the NAACP presented similar arguments. As the five cases moved toward the Supreme Court, Clarendon County Negroes paid a penalty for their boldness. Reverend DeLaine, his wife, his sisters and a number of the parents who had started the case, lost their jobs. Before the fight was over DeLaine's house and church were burned and he was forced to flee to the North. Even Judge Waring's home was stoned and he too became an exile from South Carolina.

At noon on May 17, 1954, the black-robed justices of the Supreme Court filed into the courtroom. As they disposed of routine matters, word traveled through the building. "It's coming! The decision on the school cases!" Thurgood Marshall shouldered his way through a crowd of reporters to hear Chief Justice Earl Warren read the unanimous opinion:

Thurgood Marshall, May 17, 1954

"We cannot turn the clock back to 1868 when the [Fourteenth] Amendment was adopted or even to 1896 when Plessy *vs.* Ferguson was written. We must consider public education in the light of its present place in American life.

"Does segregation of children in public schools solely on the basis of race, even though the physical facilities may be equal, deprive the children of the minority group of equal educational opportunities?

"We believe that it does.

"To separate them from others of similar age and qualifications solely because of their race generates a feeling of inferiority that may affect their hearts and minds in a way unlikely ever to be undone.

"In the field of public education the doctrine of 'separate but equal' has no place. Separate educational facilities are inherently unequal."

Walter White's face was wreathed in smiles. "It took fifty-eight years but a miracle has been passed in America today," he said. Asked how long it would take to get rid of segregated schools, Thurgood Marshall predicted, "Up to five years!"

He was wrong.

"SOME'S NICE AND SOME PICKS AT
ME AND CALLS ME 'NIGGER,'
BUT I DON'T PAY THEM NO MIND.
I CAME HERE BECAUSE IT WAS FOR
THE COLORED PEOPLE'S RIGHTS."

*Effie Irene Hudson, aged 12, describing
her first days in a Mississippi "white" school.*

CHAPTER 15

The Children's Crusade

"I Had a Right to Go"

The Supreme Court did not order the immediate closing of
all-Negro schools. Instead, school boards were told to "make
a prompt and reasonable start" toward obeying the Court's
ruling. In Washington, D.C., and in several border states,
schools were opened to all boys and girls. In the Deep South,
two voices were heard. One said NOW. The other said NEVER.

While Negro parents asked school boards to admit their
children to "white" schools, fourteen men held a meeting in
Sunflower County, Mississippi, to form the first White Citizens
Council. "We intend to make it difficult, if not impossible,"
said a Council leader, "for any Negro who advocates desegregation to find and hold a job, get credit, or renew
a mortgage."

From Mississippi, the Councils spread to Louisiana, Alabama,
Texas, Arkansas, Florida, Georgia until they claimed a membership of half a million. When Negroes signed petitions to school
boards, Council members bought advertising space in local
papers to print their names and addresses. The signers were
fired from their jobs, evicted from their homes and refused

credit at banks and stores. A Negro dentist who became president of the local NAACP had his automobile insurance suddenly cancelled. Wholesalers refused to supply a Negro gas station owner after he signed a school petition. A Negro plumber who was put out of business stopped to buy a loaf of bread on the day that his name appeared in the newspaper. Glaring at him, the grocer said, "That'll cost you a dollar." By 1955 the NAACP had to open a special account in a Negro-owned bank to lend money to families who were penalized for trying to get a better education for their children.

The Councils were only part of the story. During the first years after the Supreme Court ruling, southern legislatures passed almost two hundred new segregation laws. Virginia called for "massive resistance." Alabama declared the decision "null, void, and of no effect." Mississippi set up a State Sovereignty Commission "to prohibit compliance with the integration decisions" and Georgia made it a felony "for any school official to spend tax money for public schools in which the races are mixed." Behind the lawmakers stood the Ku Klux Klan and a host of new racist groups—the Southern Association of Red Shirts, Knights of the White Christians, White America Inc., the Christian Civil League. They were ready with kerosene-soaked crosses, dynamite sticks and rifles if all else failed.

The year 1956 saw the return of "annual autumnal outbreaks" in the South, as there had been during reconstruction. Only these outbreaks took place in the first week in September and the front-line fighters were children.

In Clay, Kentucky, ten-year-old James Gordon listened to a radio report about Negro boys and girls who were entering a "white" school. He and his eight-year-old sister, Theresa, attended an all-Negro school in Providence, eleven miles from home. "Mommy," he asked, "if they can go to that school, why can't we go to the school in Clay?"

Mrs. Gordon took a deep breath. "If you've got the guts to go, I got the guts to take you," she said.

James and Theresa had "the guts to go" even after a crowd attacked their car on the first and second days of school, almost overturning it. They went on the third day with a hundred National Guardsmen escorting them. They had the courage to stay when a girl screamed, "I'd rather be an idiot

James and Theresa Gordon

than go to school with niggers," and the white children and all
but three of the teachers left the building.

"With the crowds screaming and all, I lost my nerve," Mrs.
Gordon said. "I asked them if they wanted to go back and
they said yes. I couldn't take their courage from them so
I let them go back. I died a thousand deaths every day
until three o'clock."

While James looked out of the window of his empty classroom, sixteen-year-old Bobby Cain led a dozen Negro teen-
agers through a heckling crowd in Clinton, Tennessee. Tight-
lipped, they marched up the steps of Clinton High—"the
longest journey in our lives," they said. Inside the school,
members of a White Citizens Youth Council poured ink in
their lockers, smeared eggs on their books and followed them
through the corridors with whispered threats. At lunchtime a
group of men and boys chased Bobby down the street, rough-
ing him up until the police took him to jail for protective
custody.

"I won't say I wasn't afraid after that," Bobby said. "But
it came to me that I had a right to go to school. It was
those other people who were breaking the law, not me. I
determined to stick it out.

"At first it was pretty rough. I couldn't concentrate on my
lessons. They don't wear those White Citizens Youth buttons
any more but the other day a boy had a hangman's noose,
little twisted piece of rope he'd made, on his shirt. Another
had one in the palm of his hand, just flashed it at me in
class."

After a series of dynamite blasts shattered Negro homes and
stores in Clinton five of the boys and girls left the school,
some moving with their families to other parts of the country.
Bobby stuck it out. On the third anniversary of the Supreme
Court decision he became the first Negro to graduate from
Clinton High.

The following September nine Negro boys and girls registered at Central High School in Little Rock, Arkansas. On

opening day, National Guardsmen ringed the school with orders from Governor Faubus to keep the Negro students out.
Elizabeth Eckford, a slender fifteen-year-old, was the first to
arrive. When she got off the bus hundreds of men and women
followed her. At first all she could hear was the shuffling of
their feet. Then someone shouted, "Here she comes, get ready!"
With her head high and her knees shaking, Elizabeth walked
to the entrance of the school. Guardsmen raised their bayonets
to block her way.

"I turned around and the crowd came toward me," Elizabeth
said. "They moved closer and closer. Somebody started yelling,
'Lynch her! Lynch her!'

"I tried to see a friendly face somewhere in the mob. I
looked into the face of an old woman, but she spat on me.

"They came closer, shouting, 'No nigger is going to get in
our school. Get out of here!'

"I turned back to the guards but their faces told me I
wouldn't get help from them. Then I looked down the block
and saw a bench at the bus stop. I thought, 'If I can only
get there I will be safe.'

"When I finally got there the mob crowded up and began
shouting all over again. Someone hollered, 'Drag her over to
this tree! Let's take care of the nigger.'"

At last one white woman elbowed her way to the bench to
stand beside Elizabeth. "Why don't you leave her alone?" she
scolded. "She's only a little girl." With her help, Elizabeth
managed to board a bus and go home.

Newspaper pictures of Elizabeth Eckford in the trim new
dress she had made for her first day at school and the hate-
filled faces of the grownups who pursued her brought world-
wide sympathy to the embattled Little Rock youngsters. After
weeks of fruitless conferences with Governor Faubus, President
Eisenhower placed the Arkansas National Guard under federal
orders and sent eleven hundred paratroopers to keep order in
Little Rock.

With the armed might of the United States on their side,

Elizabeth Eckford

the nine students were able to enter Central High School. While paratroopers patrolled the corridors, a small group of their schoolmates waged a war of nerves against them—a war that ranged from kicks and shoves to the dumping of a bowl of hot soup on one girl's head.

For a year the Little Rock Nine were the best-known teenagers in the country. Interviewed by reporters, photographed by television cameramen, their ordeal was described in one editorial as "The Children's Crusade."

"These children have to walk calmly and coolly out to meet tormenting and humiliating attacks that hurt to the very soul," wrote a North Carolina college professor. "I cannot recall that there has ever been a more inspiring demonstration of courage by the children of any race, in any age. Salute them and I think others will take heart and go over and stand beside them. It may help us to believe this *is* the home of the brave, perhaps more than it is the land of the free."

"The Children's Crusade" continued in other southern cities. In Nashville, Tennessee, a dynamite blast destroyed a school where a five-year-old Negro girl was registered. In Jacksonville, Florida, a bomb wrecked the home of a six-year-old boy who had gone to a "white" school. In New Orleans the presence of four Negro first-graders touched off a year-long school boy-cott. Encouraged by the governor and the legislature, crowds surrounded the schools. Singing "Glory, Glory, Segregation" to the tune of the "Battle Hymn of the Republic," they forced white parents to take their children home.

Virginia's program of "massive resistance" closed all the schools in Norfolk, Charlottesville and Front Royal for five months until a group of parents sued to have them reopened. Schools in Prince Edward County where one of the original school cases had started remained closed for four years. Prince Edward's white children attended a "private" academy, which was supported by state grants, but the county's seventeen hundred Negro boys and girls received no education at all during this period.

The Battle of Oxford

The climax of the "autumnal outbreaks" came in 1962 when a twenty-nine-year-old Air Force veteran applied for entrance to the University of Mississippi. Nine years of integrated living in the Air Force had convinced James Meredith to return to his home state and fight for justice there. Up to the time he asked for a transfer from all-Negro Jackson State College to the all-white university, Mississippi had resisted every attempt at school desegregation. And, said Governor Ross Barnett, it would continue to do so.

After federal courts ordered Meredith's admission to the university, Barnett personally took charge of the fight to bar him. His defiance of a series of court orders forced a showdown between the state and the United States Government.

"Americans are free to disagree with the law but not to disobey it," President Kennedy declared in a nationwide television speech. "If this country should ever reach the point where any man or group of men, by force or threat of force, could long deny the commands of our courts and our Constitution, then no law would stand free from doubt, no judge would be sure of his writ, and no citizen would be safe from his neighbors."

The President was still on the air appealing to the people of Mississippi when federal marshals brought James Meredith to the university campus at Oxford. They were met by twenty-five hundred students and adults who had come from all over the state. Waving Confederate flags they attacked the marshals with bricks, gasoline bombs and guns. Cars were burned, windows broken, street lights shot out. Meredith was safely installed in a dormitory room but the battle raged for fifteen hours, until battalions of U.S. soldiers put down the uprising with tear gas and smoke grenades. When it was over, almost four hundred had been injured and two were dead. One of the men killed by a stray bullet was a French reporter who wrote in his last dispatch, "The Civil War has never ended."

The civil war against the Supreme Court's ruling didn't end on the University of Mississippi campus, but the Battle of Oxford was the last pitched battle. James Meredith spent his college days under the watchful eyes of soldiers and marshals. Outfitted with guns and walkie-talkies, they shared his meals and dormitory room and escorted him to classes. By the time he graduated new voices were speaking in the South. Instead of NEVER! they were saying "soon" and "maybe" and "a few." Massive resistance had collapsed. In its place school boards were trying token desegregation—the admission of small numbers of Negroes to "white" schools.

Freedom of Choice

Ten years after the Supreme Court said, "Separate educational facilities are unequal," Negro children were attending mixed schools in every state in the South. Their numbers were microscopic, however. Fifty-seven black Mississippians went to schools with white children. The figure for Alabama was 101, for South Carolina, 265. Altogether 2.25 per cent of the Negro boys and girls in southern states were in desegregated schools. That left 2,876,967 students who were continuing to receive an inferior education.

In Clarendon County the boys and girls whose names appeared on the first school petition had grown up, married and had children of their own. And their children were going to segregated schools. There were no Negroes in Clarendon County's "white" schools in 1964. The following year the number jumped from zero to one. "At the rate we're moving," Negro parents told the school board in Little Rock, "we won't have integration for 450 years."

Some progress has been made since then. A Civil Rights Act passed by Congress in 1964 gave the U. S. Commissioner of Education the power to cut off federal money from school districts that failed to work out plans for integration. Although this power has since been limited, the possibility of losing badly needed funds has speeded up desegregation. Law schools and medical schools no longer discriminate against Negro applicants. Southern colleges have begun to seek out the brightest Negro high schoolers as well as the best athletes, and even the University of Mississippi enrolled seventy Negroes last year. Teachers' organizations are integrating and in scattered places in the South, Negroes are teaching white pupils for the first time.

Progress has been made but two school systems still exist and the "freedom of choice" plan that most school boards use puts the burden of desegregation on Negro parents and their children. On the face of it, "freedom of choice" sounds democratic.

Parents may select which school they want their children to attend. In practice a parent who chooses the "white" school is subject to all sorts of intimidation.

In Carthage, Mississippi, A. J. Lewis and his wife chose Carthage Elementary School for their six-year-old daughter. One day after Debra went to school with her white neighbors, Mr. Lewis was fired from his job. Then "the merchants wouldn't sell us anything. We couldn't even get gas from any gas station," Mrs. Lewis said. "For the first three or four months we didn't sleep at night because we had to guard the house." In spite of their nightly patrol two fires were set and their landlord told them to move.

Nevertheless Debra stayed in school. "Somebody had to do it," her mother explained. "If we had turned around I don't think desegregation ever could have gotten started here." As a result of their pioneering, other families braved the white com-

Negro parents in New Rochelle

munity. By the time Debra was in third grade, thirty black youngsters were going to Carthage Elementary School.

The Lewises faced only economic pressure. Many Negro parents have listened to their children scream, "Stop! Stop!" as they dreamed at night of the beatings they received during the day. A doctor who examined black boys and girls who had chosen the white high school in Camden, Alabama, found them "shell-shocked" because of "extreme physical harassment" by their schoolmates. Often this harassment takes place on the school bus or in the classroom and the adults in charge do nothing to stop it.

The ugliest of all the "autumnal disturbances" occurred in Grenada, Mississippi, in 1966. Grown men, armed with ax handles, lead pipes and chains, attacked boys and girls as they left Horn Elementary School on opening day.

"Now you going to come back to this school again?" a man asked, after kicking and beating a twelve-year-old. The sobbing boy who promised that he would not return was hardly exercising his freedom of choice.

Segregation Northern Style

New Rochelle, New York, is a suburban community a thousand miles from Mississippi. After the Supreme Court decision its citizens followed the civil rights struggle with clear consciences. Certainly there was no segregation in New Rochelle. Children attended elementary schools in their neighborhoods. After sixth grade, they went to one of the two junior highs and then on to New Rochelle High, the only senior high in the city.

Everyone was happy about New Rochelle's schools except the parents of Negro children, who began to appear at school board meetings in increasing numbers. Their main complaint was Lincoln Elementary School, the oldest school in the city.

Lincoln's sixty-year-old building was dilapidated, its course of study outdated—and 94 per cent of its pupils were black. Since Negroes made up only 13 per cent of the population of New Rochelle it seemed clear to Lincoln parents that their children were segregated.

The school board heard this charge with surprise and growing resentment. You won't find discrimination here, they said. After all, New Rochelle outlawed segregated schools back in 1889. Yes, 94 per cent was a pretty high figure but that was because Lincoln was in a Negro neighborhood. Regrettable perhaps but nothing that the board could change.

As the debates at meetings grew sharper, the school board proposed to replace Lincoln School with a new $1.3 million building—on the same street. Lincoln parents campaigned against this, pointing out that the new school would only continue segregation, but a majority of New Rochelle's voters approved the proposal. It was then that the Negro parents made a now-or-never decision.

In the first week of September in 1960, a determined band of mothers took their children to "white" elementary schools in New Rochelle. There was no violence. Just a polite, "Sorry, your child belongs in the Lincoln School district. You'll have to go there." The mothers refused. For a year their children were tutored in the home of a Negro social worker while the parents hired a lawyer and went to court.

A federal judge found New Rochelle's school board guilty of segregating its elementary schools. Although the board had avoided mentioning "Negro," its school district lines were carefully drawn to keep black children in Lincoln. The few white youngsters who lived in the district were allowed to transfer elsewhere, but Negroes were denied this opportunity. The judge was particularly critical of the plan to build a new building next door to the old one. "If a board of education selects a school site or otherwise operates its school with purposeful desire to segregate or to maintain segregation, the Constitution has been violated," he ruled. "It is of no moment whether

the segregation is labeled as *de jure* [by law] or *de facto* [in fact] as long as the board is responsible for its maintenance."

New Rochelle's school board fought the decision all the way to the Supreme Court and lost. Board members resigned. PTA meetings turned into name-calling sessions. After years of wrangling, the doors of Lincoln Elementary School were locked and its pupils were assigned to "white" schools.

Meanwhile, the country had learned a new phrase—*de facto* segregation. In front of schools in the North and West, mothers carried signs: END DE FACTO SEGREGATION . . . SCHOOL SEGREGATION—WE HAVE IT TOO . . . OUR SCHOOL IS INFERIOR, OUR CHILDREN ARE NOT.

Negro parents had always known that the ghetto schools their children attended were not doing a proper teaching job. Now the New Rochelle case spurred them to organize. They started school boycotts in New Jersey, picket lines in Chicago, "freedom schools" in Boston, sit-ins in New York.

White Northerners read the picket signs with a sense of shock. "Who, me?" they asked when Negroes accused them of discrimination. They were not responsible for the fact that millions of Negroes were still pouring into northern cities. They had always deplored southern attitudes on race. Nor could they be blamed for the movement of millions of whites to the suburbs. The white parents were only looking for trees and fresh air, and perhaps a better education for their children. It wasn't anyone's fault that city schools that had once been integrated were now nearly all black. Nevertheless, the schools were *in fact* segregated and the youngsters who attended them were being shortchanged.

"The teachers, they don't care about teaching no Negro children," said a boy who joined a boycott of New York schools in 1964. "Like my teacher, he says 'I don't care if you don't learn. I'm getting paid for it anyway.' When I was in a class with white children a teacher never said that. They all taught. Everybody learned the same thing."

"Once a white kid's sitting next to a colored kid," a girl agreed, "that teacher's going to have to teach. And when he teaches you're going to have to learn some way or the other."

"Besides," another boy said, "you go to an all-white school, you see them sitting up there with brand-new books and you go to a *de facto* segregated school and see them sitting with raggedy books, taped up covers and everything. Everybody gets tired of this. Everybody can't stand raggedy things."

Prodded by picket lines and court orders—and sometimes by conscience and concern—school boards have desegregated schools in a number of communities. After World War II, Princeton, New Jersey, had two elementary schools, one almost all white, the other Negro. The school board merged the two schools, assigning pupils from kindergarten to fifth grade to one and sixth- to eighth-graders to the other. As a result, all of Princeton's boys and girls attended classes together. The Princeton Plan has been adopted in towns from New York to California. Other communities, learning a lesson from New Rochelle, have replaced schools in ghetto neighborhoods with new centrally located buildings. Still others plan educational parks which will bring all of a city's children together on one campus, similar to a college campus. By concentrating libraries, language labs, and even theater and concert halls, they hope to have quality as well as integrated education.

In big cities where there are hundreds of schools, thousands of pupils, and ghetto areas that sprawl over many miles, desegregation has been less successful. Countless meetings have been held, countless plans have been put down on paper, but few have been put into action. Although the problems are complex, indifference and prejudice also play a part in the slowdown.

New York City's Board of Education, in 1964, proposed to pair forty-two schools, along the lines of the Princeton Plan. The proposal would have reduced segregation in the city by only 1 per cent. Nevertheless it touched off an uproar. White parents formed Parents and Taxpayers (PAT) groups to oppose "busing" children out of their neighborhoods. The longest bus ride involved was slightly more than a mile and would have taken ten minutes. Since almost one hundred thousand New York children go to school by bus, some riding for an hour each way, this hardly seemed a hardship. Yet PAT won such widespread sympathy that the Board of Education cut the number of paired schools from forty-two to eight. In Chicago where defense of the "neighborhood school" and opposition to "busing" has been even louder, all attempts at desegregation have failed.

At the request of President Johnson, the U. S. Commission on Civil Rights did a study of "Racial Isolation in the Public Schools." Their report, issued in 1967, makes dismal reading. Nine out of ten of the Negro children in Chicago and St. Louis attend elementary schools that are almost all black. In Cleveland, the figure is 82 per cent, in Philadelphia and Detroit, 72 per cent. In spite of court decisions, in spite of Negro protests, segregation in the big city schools of the North is on the increase. The vast majority of black children in the United States go to schools that are separate and unequal.

"THESE STUDENTS ARE NOT STRUGGLING FOR THEMSELVES ALONE.
THEY ARE SEEKING TO SAVE THE SOUL OF AMERICA.
THEY ARE TAKING OUR WHOLE NATION BACK
TO THOSE GREAT WELLS OF DEMOCRACY
WHICH WERE DUG DEEP BY THE FOUNDING FATHERS.
IN SITTING DOWN AT THE LUNCH COUNTERS,
THEY ARE IN REALITY STANDING UP
FOR THE BEST IN THE AMERICAN DREAM."

Martin Luther King, Jr., 1961

CHAPTER 16

Soul Power

Please Be Peaceful

"Please be peaceful. We are not advocating violence. I want you to love our enemies."

The man was speaking from the shattered porch of his home. A half hour earlier a bomb had exploded, breaking his front windows and endangering the lives of his wife and baby daughter. The noise of the explosion had brought an angry crowd to his yard. Armed with rocks and guns, they were threatening the police and city officials who had come to survey the damage.

"We must love our white brothers no matter what they do to us," the man continued. "If I am stopped, this movement will not stop, for what we are doing is right. What we are doing is just—and God is with us."

As he finished there were murmured "Amens." "God bless you, son," a woman said in a tearful voice. Slowly and thoughtfully Montgomery's Negroes drifted toward their homes.

"I'll be honest with you," a policeman told a reporter. "I

was terrified. I owe my life to that preacher and so do all the other white people who were there."

The preacher was Martin Luther King, Jr. On the January night in 1956 when his home was bombed he gave the Negro movement and the nation a new philosophy. The son of a minister, King had grown up in the segregated city of Atlanta, Georgia. As a boy he had been troubled by the conflict between Jesus' command to "love thy neighbor" and the hatred and oppression he saw around him. How could he love a Klansman or a lyncher? And if he turned the other cheek to injustice when would it ever stop?

He was fifteen when he read Henry David Thoreau's essay on "Civil Disobedience." A hundred years earlier Thoreau had refused to pay his taxes because the tax money would have supported the Fugitive Slave Law and an "unnecessary and unjust" war with Mexico. Instead he went to jail.

"Unjust laws exist," Thoreau wrote. "Shall we be content to obey them, or shall we endeavor to amend them, and obey them until we have succeeded, or shall we transgress them at once?"

His answer was, "If the injustice requires you to be the agent of injustice to another, then, I say, break the law." If a thousand or even a hundred men would obey their consciences and disobey unjust laws, they could bring about "a peaceable revolution."

Impressed with the idea of refusing to co-operate with an evil system, King read and reread "Civil Disobedience." When he went north to graduate school he learned of Mahatma Gandhi, the Indian leader who had put Thoreau's ideas into practice. During a thirty-year struggle to free India from British rule, Gandhi and his followers boycotted, fasted, marched and went to jail until they won their peaceable revolution.

Gandhi's civil disobedience campaigns were based on what he called *satyagraha*—"the force contained in truth and love." This was the "soul power" which enabled Indians to face brutal punishments without fighting back. By breaking unjust laws

Martin Luther King

and suffering the consequences Gandhi believed that they could appeal to the consciences of the lawmakers. Nonviolent resistance, he told his countrymen, was an "all-sided sword" that "blesses him who uses it and him against whom it is used, without drawing a drop of blood."

These ideas were still swirling around in Martin Luther King's mind when, at twenty-five, he went to Montgomery to become pastor of the Dexter Avenue Baptist Church. A year later came the bus boycott touched off by Rosa Parks. Elected president of the Montgomery Improvement Association, Dr. King faced a heavy responsibility. The possibility of a clash between Negroes and whites was always present. Even before the bombing of his home, car-pool drivers had been harassed and the leaders of the MIA had received phone calls and letters threatening their lives. Nor were all the threats on one side. A member of King's church proposed that they "kill off" some white people. "This is the only language these white folks will understand," he said. "If we fail to do this they will think we're afraid. We must show them we're not afraid any longer."

As a minister, Dr. King was opposed to violence. As a black man, he knew that if a battle started, Negroes were sure to get the worst of it. All three city commissioners were members of the White Citizens Council and the mayor and the police were committed to their "get tough" policy.

At early meetings of the MIA, Dr. King pointed out that the use of force was both impractical and immoral. "Our oppressors would be happy if we resorted to violence. Our method will be that of persuasion, not coercion. We must hear the words of Jesus: 'Love your enemies, bless them that curse you, and pray for them that despitefully use you.' In spite of mistreatment we must not become bitter and end up hating our white brothers."

This was practical Christianity. It was not yet Gandhism. Only as the boycott continued did King realize the strength of nonviolent resistance. The bombing of his home was a turning point. Black Montgomery had been ready to shed blood that night. When people put away their arms they proved themselves stronger than their enemies. The whites controlled the city government, the courts, the police, the press. Against this array of might, the Negroes had their unity and determination, their willingness to suffer and courage to endure. They had "soul power."

The discovery of "soul power" had a transforming effect on Dr. King and his followers. "We got our heads up now," a man proudly told a reporter, "and we won't ever bow down again." Meanwhile white Montgomery continued to blunder. There were other bombings—and the Negroes remained peaceful. There were mass arrests—and on the morning that Dr. King came to trial Negroes crowded into the streets around the court-house. On the lapels of their coats they wore small crosses which said, "Father, forgive them."

The dignity and restraint of the bus boycotters brought them support from the rest of the country. Even in Montgomery, Gandhi's "all-sided sword" began to change people. Although the Kings still received thirty to forty threatening letters each day occasionally there would be a note saying, "Carry on, we are with you," signed, "A white friend."

Three weeks after the bus boycott was won, more than a hundred Southerners, most of them Negro ministers, met in Atlanta, Georgia, to discuss the fight for freedom. Out of this meeting came the Southern Christian Leadership Conference (SCLC) whose goals were "full citizenship rights and total integration of the Negro into American life." With Martin Luther King as president, SCLC called on Negroes to "assert their human dignity" by refusing "further cooperation with evil . . . We call upon them to understand that non-violence is not a symbol of weakness or cowardice, but as Jesus demonstrated, non-violent resistance transforms weakness into strength and breeds courage in the face of danger." In its first years SCLC supported bus boycotts in Tallahassee, Florida, Atlanta, and other southern towns, and joined with the NAACP in a campaign to register millions of Negro voters.

Meanwhile Dr. King became a national figure, speaking at so many meetings around the country that *Life* described him as "the traveling salesman of Negro rights." He went to Ghana in 1957 to take part in its Independence Day celebration and two years later made a pilgrimage to India. A visit to Gandhi's tomb and long talks with Prime Minister Jawaharlal Nehru strengthened his belief in "soul power." After his return from India he resigned his pastorate in Montgomery and moved to Atlanta. As copastor of his father's church he would have more time for civil rights. "I am convinced," he said as he left

Students sit in

Montgomery, "that the psychological moment has come when a concentrated drive against injustice can bring great tangible gains. We must employ new methods of struggle, involving the masses of the people."

The Young and the Brave

The psychological moment came at exactly four forty-five in the afternoon of February 1, 1960. In Greensboro, North Carolina, four freshmen from Agricultural and Technical College, an all-Negro school, entered a downtown Woolworth's. After buying some toothpaste they sat down at the lunch counter.

"Coffee, please," one of them said.

The waitress shook her head. "I'm sorry but we don't serve colored here."

The students remained seated at the counter until the store closed. The following morning they returned. When they left to go to their classes, others took their place.

"Segregation makes me feel unwanted," seventeen-year-old Joseph McNeill explained to a reporter who asked why he was sitting-in. "I don't want my children exposed to it." "We talked about it long enough," his roommate added. "We decided to do something."

At the end of the week more than a hundred Negroes were sitting at lunch counters in Greensboro. In Durham, fifty-five miles away, students at North Carolina College heard about the sit-in on the radio and started one of their own. From there the idea leapfrogged to Nashville and Knoxville, Tennessee, to Rock Hill and Orangeburg, South Carolina, to Jacksonville, Florida, and Atlanta, Georgia. By spring students were demonstrating in every southern and border state.

A large-scale civil disobedience campaign against Jim Crow laws was under way. Nobody called it that at first but everyone knew that the sit-inners wanted more than a cup of coffee in a dime store. Although the protest had started without any central direction, a definite pattern was emerging. Everywhere the students were neat, orderly, polite. In Nashville they followed mimeographed instructions:

> *Do show yourself friendly at all times.*
> *Do sit straight and face the counter.*
> *Don't strike back if attacked.*
> *Don't laugh out.*
> *Don't hold conversations.*

In Orangeburg they attended classes in nonviolence, learning how to protect their heads and vital organs if they were beaten. In Tallahassee they held drills. "One acts like a white man, blowing smoke in the eyes of the others and calling them all sorts of names," a girl said. "That way they learn that, regardless of what the other person does, they're just to sit there."

"You can duck a lick," a boy interrupted.

"Oh, of course," she agreed. "You can duck but you aren't to strike back."

"We had a girl in front of Kress," said a student from Raleigh, North Carolina. "A man slapped her face and took away her picket sign. He broke her glasses so she couldn't see to identify him. She came back to the campus. We asked her what she wanted to do, and she said she guessed she'd turn the other cheek, so we gave her another picket sign and she went back."

On television screens, the country saw these youngsters being pulled off stools, spat on, kicked, burned with cigarettes. It watched them pick themselves up again and sit with folded arms, not striking back. Some students in the North picketed chain stores in their communities with signs reading, WE WALK SO THEY MAY SIT. Others headed South. White students in the South joined the Negroes. Even white adults were strangely moved. The Richmond, Virginia, *News Leader*, normally pro-segregationist, said in an editorial on February 22:

Many a Virginian must have felt a tinge of wry regret at the state of things in reading of Saturday's sitdowns. Here were the colored students, in coats, white shirts, ties, and one of them was reading Goethe and one was taking notes from a biology text. And here, on the sidewalk outside, was a gang of white boys come to heckle, a ragtail rabble, slack-jawed, black-jacketed, grinning fit to kill. Eheu! It gives one pause.

But it was the students themselves who were most affected by their new-found "soul power." During a march in downtown

Atlanta a girl turned a beaming face to a television camera to tell of "the raw feeling of goodness" that the demonstration gave her. "I have never felt so intense, alive, such a sense of well-being," another student wrote. They were a part of The Movement, always written with capital letters, and they were young, brave, hopeful—and sure they were right. They sang as they marched, taking over old hymns and union songs, adding new words of their own. They sang the "Ballad of the Student Sit-Ins" and "Freedom's Comin' and It Won't Be Long." Most often they linked hands and sang "We Shall Overcome."

Store managers posted signs on their lunch counters: CLOSED FOR REPAIRS . . . CLOSED IN THE INTEREST OF PUBLIC SAFETY. Police arrested the sit-inners for trespassing and unlawful assembly. In jail, they studied their textbooks and read *The Life of Mahatma Gandhi* while the cell blocks rang with "We Shall Overcome."

The Movement pushed forward rapidly. Department stores were boycotted. There were sit-ins in art galleries, walk-ins in parks, kneel-ins to integrate churches and prayer meetings on the steps of city halls. There were stand-ins in movie theaters, read-ins in segregated libraries and wade-ins at "whites-only" beaches and pools.

After meetings with Negro spokesmen, merchants in Nashville, Atlanta, San Antonio took down their CLOSED signs and opened their lunch counters to all. Memphis allowed Negroes to visit its zoo—but Danville, Virginia, closed its public library rather than obey a court order to integrate. By the fall of 1960 almost a hundred cities had quietly integrated restaurants and other public places. "I used to say this town was not ready for desegregation," a Nashville businessman said. "The sit-ins made it ready."

As the sit-ins spread, adults came forward to help the students. Six weeks after the first sit-in in Greensboro, more than a thousand Negroes had been arrested. Calling a meeting of lawyers, the NAACP drew up a master plan to defend the young people and raise money for bail. "We are going to appeal every fine," Thurgood Marshall promised. "Arrest by the police or conviction by the courts is state enforcement of private discrimination and is in violation of the Fourteenth Amendment."

While the NAACP took on the burden of legal defense Dr. King and his aides worked to bring the protesters together in some sort of continuing organization. On Easter weekend, SCLC arranged a conference in Raleigh, North Carolina. Forty southern campuses were represented and nineteen northern colleges sent delegates. Dr. King spoke to them about nonviolence not only as a method for integrating lunch counters but as a way to change the hearts of segregationists. "Our ultimate end," he said, "must be the creation of the beloved community."

The students looked up to Dr. King as their "spiritual father" but they decided to remain independent of SCLC. Before the conference ended—one enthusiastic delegate called it "the most significant gathering ever held in America since the Constitutional Convention"—they formed the Student Nonviolent Coordinating Committee.

A month later SNCC—pronounced Snick—opened an office in Atlanta and issued a statement of purpose. In words that echoed King's, the statement affirmed, "the ideal of nonviolence," with love as its central theme. "Such love . . . remains loving and forgiving even in the midst of hostility. It matches the capacity of evil to inflict suffering with an even more enduring capacity to absorb evil, all the while persisting in love. By appealing to conscience . . . nonviolence nurtures the atmosphere in which reconciliation and justice become actual possibilities."

Freedom Ride

The Congress of Racial Equality (CORE) also moved into the limelight with the sit-ins. CORE was started during World

War II by James Farmer and a handful of graduate students from the University of Chicago. Farmer, the then twenty-two-year-old son of a Negro college professor, had studied for the ministry. After receiving his degree he decided that he could not "honestly preach the Gospel of Christ in a church that practiced discrimination." Instead he went to work for the Fellowship of Reconciliation, a pacifist group. Reading the works of Gandhi and his followers, he drew up a plan for an interracial organization which would use Gandhi's methods to attack segregation. With a go-ahead from the Fellowship he set up a pilot project in Chicago.

On a spring night in 1942 Farmer and a white friend were talking over the new organization. They stopped for a cup of coffee in the Jack Sprat, a restaurant near the university. The restaurant manager was reluctant to serve Negroes. When he tried to charge twenty-five cents for a five-cent doughnut, CORE had found its first project. Farmer and his friend returned to the Jack Sprat a few days later. This time the manager threw their money at them and screamed, "Get out!"

Using Gandhi's writings as their rule book, they tried to reason with the manager. After telephone calls, letters and interviews failed to influence him, the group decided on direct action. At dinnertime when the restaurant was at its busiest, twenty-five CORE members entered and took seats. A waitress brought food to the white demonstrators but told the Negroes to go to the basement. The group sat there, their food untouched. The restaurant grew crowded, the manager more and more upset. When his regular customers began to leave because no tables were available, he was forced to give in.

CORE grew slowly after its first successful sit-in. Chapters were formed in St. Louis, Baltimore, New York. They desegregated swimming pools, skating rinks, restaurants and sponsored summer workshops to teach the principles of nonviolence. Until the Montgomery bus boycott, Farmer said, "We were small, northern, middle-class, idealistic and predominantly white."

After Dr. King focused national attention on nonviolence,

Freedom riders' bus burns

CORE was able to open a small office in downtown New York and hire its first paid workers. When the student sit-ins began, the organization was swamped with calls for help. As the only group in the country with years of experience in nonviolent direct action, its staff members worked around the clock giving advice and planning strategy. They set up the first training sessions, teaching the students to sit with hands unclenched, without showing anger, when attacked. And it was typical of their idealism to remind the sit-inners to leave a tip for the waitress who refused to serve them. "After all," a CORE leader pointed out, "she shouldn't suffer. It's not her fault."

CORE members' patience and love were sorely tested the following year. In December 1960, the Supreme Court ruled that restaurants and waiting rooms in bus terminals could not be segregated. In order to put the Court's ruling into practice, CORE decided on a "Freedom Ride" from Washington, D.C., to New Orleans. On May 4, 1961, seven Negro and six white CORE members boarded buses in Washington. At each stop they ate at lunch counters together and used "white" waiting rooms. The ride proceeded more or less peacefully until the buses entered Alabama. Outside of Anniston one bus was ambushed and set afire. As the Freedom Riders escaped from the blazing bus, they were attacked by a mob.

There and in Birmingham they were savagely beaten. One white man was dragged into an alley and worked over with fists and pipes until his face was a bloody pulp. The next day, with bandaged heads and blackened eyes, the riders continued. But they were no longer only thirteen.

When photographs of the bus burning and beatings appeared in the newspapers, others flocked to join them. "There are young folks coming in from all over," a minister in Montgomery marveled. "From Washington, Nashville, New Orleans. Thirty arrived last night and more are on the way." Another mob attack in Montgomery increased the size of the movement. "These beatings cannot deter us," a Rider spoke from his hospital bed. "We want only equality and justice and we will get it. We are prepared to die."

Throughout the spring and summer, Freedom Riders crossed the South on buses, trains and planes. College students came from as far away as California and the state of Washington. Ministers, teachers, housewives, braved beatings and arrests to enter segregated waiting rooms. In Mississippi alone more than three hundred Freedom Riders were jailed. There they had their first encounter with "wrist breakers," special handcuffs with a protruding screw that dug into their arms. They writhed on the floors of their cells in pain, but they managed to keep on singing.

While hundreds rode the buses, thousands cheered them on. In New York a part-time Freedom Rider who was a full-time history professor said that if asked, "What did you do for the liberation of your fellow man?" he would answer with some pride, "In June 1961 I took a bus ride to Florida."

By fall the Interstate Commerce Commission was ready with a sweeping order that forbade discrimination on interstate buses, trains and in bus and railroad stations. The railings between Negro and white waiting rooms were removed. The WHITE and COLORED signs came down. The right to ride which Negroes had been seeking for more than a century was fully established.

"WHEN I GO NEAR A VOTING REGISTRAR IN MISSISSIPPI
I FEEL LIKE I'M DUELING WITH THE WHOLE HISTORY
OF MY RACE AND THE WHITE RACE.
IT GETS YOU JUST LIKE THAT, IN YOUR BONES.
YOU'RE NOT JUST A PERSON WHO IS SCARED.
YOU'RE DOING SOMETHING FOR THE BOOKS, FOR HISTORY."

A Negro student, 1964

CHAPTER 17

"...Because It Is Right"

Project C

In 1963 the United States celebrated the one hundredth anniversary of the Emancipation Proclamation. "That Proclamation was only a first step," President Kennedy said in a special message to Congress. "Through these long one hundred years, progress for the Negro has been too often blocked and delayed. The harmful, wasteful and wrongful results of racial discrimination still appear in virtually every aspect of national life, in virtually every part of the Nation."

No one knew this better than the Negroes of Birmingham, Alabama. One hundred years after the Emancipation Proclamation, Birmingham's laws forbade "the mixing of the races" in any public place. The Supreme Court had said that schools must be integrated. Birmingham's schools were segregated. The Supreme Court had said that parks must be integrated. Birmingham closed its parks, playgrounds and golf courses in reply. The Interstate Commerce Commission had ruled that bus stations could not discriminate. The manager of Birmingham's bus station had been arrested when he desegregated its lunch counter. The drinking fountains in Birmingham's City

Hall were still labeled WHITE and COLORED. So were its
taxicabs, ambulances, hospital wards.

Birmingham was the largest industrial city in the South.
One hundred and fifty thousand of its citizens were black,
yet the foremen in the steel mills, the clerks in offices, the
salesmen in stores, the policemen, firemen, bus drivers, jurors
were never anything but white. One hundred years after the
Emancipation Proclamation, a black woman buying a dress
in a Birmingham department store could not go into a fitting
room to try it on. In stores and offices she was addressed
by her first name, never as "Mrs. Jones."

Birmingham was a Klan city where more than fifty bombings of Negro homes and churches remained unsolved crimes.
Negroes called it "Bombingham." Police Commissioner "Bull"
Connor was known throughout the country for his racism. In
one interview Connor told a reporter, "Damn the law. Down
here I am the Law."

Meeting in the Negro-owned Gaston Motel on Fifth Avenue
North, Reverend Fred Shuttlesworth, founder of the Alabama
Christian Movement for Human Rights, Martin Luther King
and Reverend Wyatt Tee Walker, SCLC's executive director,
made plans for Project C. "C" stood for confrontation—the
face-to-face encounter of black Birmingham with the white
community. Its goal was an "open city" where all public
services and facilities would be open to Negroes equally with
whites.

While King traveled north to alert other civil rights organizations and raise money for bail, Shuttlesworth and Walker put
the final touches on Project C. Pacing off the distances from
the Sixteenth Street Baptist Church and the Gaston Motel to
City Hall, they planned the best routes for marches. In downtown stores, they mapped entrances and exits, even counting
stools and tables in lunchrooms to determine how many demonstrators would be needed in each place. They met with lawyers,
set up a transportation corps and trained an army of volunteers.
Every volunteer signed a "commitment blank" which began,

"I hereby pledge myself—my person and body—to the non-violent movement."

On April 3 when Easter shopping was at its peak, Project C went into action. Black men and women quietly sat down at lunch counters in department stores. Outside, pickets walked, urging Negroes not to buy in the stores. "Wear old clothes for Easter," they said. Then came marches to City Hall, parades to the county building to register to vote, pray-ins at churches on Sundays. Day after day the demonstrations grew larger. Hundreds were jailed, including Martin Luther King, and hundreds came forward to take their place.

On May 3 laughing, singing groups of young people filed out of the Sixteenth Street Baptist Church. Police and firemen lay in wait. As the marchers headed downtown, streams of water from high-pressure hoses sent them sprawling. Those who managed to dodge the hoses met "Bull" Connor's second line of attack—dogs. A photograph of a police dog lunging at the throat of a boy united black Birmingham and outraged millions of people.

The demonstrations increased in intensity. On May 7, twenty-five hundred men, women and children poured into the streets. "Turn on your water, turn loose your dogs, we will stand here till we die," a minister cried. A thousand people were arrested and the following day three thousand faced the police lines to chant "Freedom, freedom." An armored car roared to and fro, forcing the marchers back. A stream of water hurled Reverend Shuttlesworth against a church wall, injuring his chest. When an ambulance took him to the hospital "Bull" Connor said, "I wish they'd carried him away in a hearse."

The confrontation between Connor's men, wielding clubs and hoses, and the nonviolent demonstrators was happening before the eyes of the whole world. Newsmen were there from Europe, Asia, Africa and from all over the United States. Project C again forced the country to look at the ugly facts of racism. Shocked by what they saw, people backed the marchers and protested to the President. Before the week was out Burke

Birmingham, Alabama, 1963

Marshall, chief of the Civil Rights Division of the Department of Justice, flew from Washington to arrange a truce. He talked to downtown merchants whose stores were empty. Some realized, one man said, "that what the Negroes were demanding wasn't so unreasonable—to have a cup of coffee at a lunch counter, to get a decent job."

Telephone calls from President Kennedy and the chairman of the board of U. S. Steel, Birmingham's largest industry, did the rest. After an all-night meeting, business leaders—but not the mayor or governor—gave in to many of the Negroes' demands. While the mayor called them "a bunch of gutless traitors" the businessmen agreed to desegregate lunch counters, fitting rooms, drinking fountains in downtown stores. Negroes were to be hired for "front of the store" jobs. A biracial committee was set up as a "channel of communications" between the races.

"The city of Birmingham has come to an accord with its conscience," Dr. King and Reverend Shuttlesworth announced.

They were too optimistic. The pact was one day old when the Ku Klux Klan held a cross burning on the outskirts of the city. "King should be met with force," a speaker said. "We need to go back to the old-time Klan." After the meeting broke up, dynamite explosions wrecked the home of Reverend A. D. King, Martin Luther King's brother. Shortly afterward the Gaston Motel was bombed.

The bombings touched off a riot in the Negro section of the city. Enraged men who had never signed nonviolence pledges threw bricks and bottles at the police, smashed their patrol cars and set fires. At dawn, Birmingham settled down to an uneasy peace.

I Have a Dream

In the summer of '63, the Negroes of America began to write their own Emancipation Proclamation. From Cambridge, Maryland, to St. Augustine, Florida, from Danville, Virginia, to Amarillo, Texas—in eight hundred cities and towns—they marched, picketed, sat-in. Every Negro civil rights organization and many white groups took part in The Movement.

"My objectivity went out the window when I saw a picture of those cops sitting on that woman and holding her down by the throat," said Roy Wilkins, the NAACP's soft-spoken executive secretary. He flew to Mississippi, picketed Woolworth's—and went to jail.

"Some time or other, we are all going to have to stand and be on the receiving end of a fire hose," said Dr. Eugene Carson Blake, who subsequently became general secretary of the World

Council of Churches. With other ministers and rabbis, Dr. Blake attempted to integrate an amusement park in Baltimore— and went to jail.

James Farmer of CORE barely escaped lynching in Plaquemine, Louisiana, after he led a protest march to City Hall. Young field workers from SNCC were shot and beaten in Mississippi when they tried to help black men and women register to vote.

The climax of the summer came after A. Philip Randolph, spirited elder statesman of the civil rights movement, proposed a March on Washington. On August 28, a quarter of a million Americans, including many thousands of whites, paraded to the mall in front of the Lincoln Memorial with signs saying, FREEDOM NOW, JOBS AND FREEDOM, WE MARCH FOR INTEGRATED SCHOOLS. The sun shone from a cloudless sky as the marchers staged the largest and most peaceful demonstration that the capital had ever seen. "The sweetness and patience of the crowd," reported the New York *Times*, "may have set some sort of national high-water mark in mass decency."

It was a day of cheers and sadness, of recollections of the past and hopes for the future. With tear-stained cheeks, Marian Anderson once again sang from the steps of the Lincoln Memorial. Rosa Parks was introduced to the audience. A. Philip Randolph talked of the March-That-Never-Was and of marches still-to-be "until freedom is ours." Roy Wilkins paid tribute to W. E. B. Du Bois who had died the night before at the age of ninety-five. Whitney Young spoke for the Urban League and James Farmer, unavoidably detained, sent a message from a Louisiana jail.

John Lewis of SNCC sounded an angry note. "We are tired of being beaten up by policemen. We're tired of having our people locked up in jail. You holler, 'Be patient,'" he told white America. "We want our freedom and we want it now."

The last speaker was Martin Luther King. His deep resounding voice moved listeners to tears as he told of his dream: "I have a dream—that my four little children will one day

March on Washington, 1963

live in a nation where they will not be judged by the color of their skin but by their character.

"I have a dream—that one day, on the red hills of Georgia the sons of slaves and the sons of slaveowners will sit together at the table of brotherhood.

"I have a dream—that one day, even the state of Mississippi will be transformed into an oasis of freedom and justice.

"This will be the day when all of God's children will be able to sing with new meaning, 'My country 'tis of thee, sweet land of liberty, . . . let freedom ring.'

"When we let freedom ring from every village and every hamlet, from every state and every city, black men and white men, Jews and Gentiles, Protestants and Catholics, will be able to join hands and sing in the words of the old Negro spiritual:

> *Free at last,*
> *Free at last.*
> *Thank God Almighty*
> *We are free at last.*"

In 1963, three hundred southern cities agreed to some desegregation of public places, some jobs for Negroes. In small towns in southeastern Louisiana, black men voted for the first time since 1902. In Mississippi where 98 per cent of the state's Negro citizens were still denied the ballot, civil rights workers organized a Freedom Ballot campaign. While whites voted for Paul Johnson for governor in the fall elections, eighty-five thousand black Mississippians who were not permitted to register cast Freedom Ballots for Aaron Henry, president of the state NAACP. The Freedom Ballots were not official, of course, but they proved that Negroes in Mississippi were determined to use their right to vote if they had the chance. The size of the vote was also something for the national leaders of both political parties to think about.

Early in the year, President Kennedy had asked Congress to pass a mild civil rights bill. After Birmingham, he proposed a new law that would forbid discrimination in public places, outlaw racial barriers in employment and speed up the desegregation of schools. "Justice requires us to insure the blessings of liberty for all Americans," he said. "Not merely for reasons of economic efficiency, world diplomacy and domestic tranquillity—but above all because it is right."

His proposed law, passed after his death, became the Civil Rights Act of 1964.

"Soul power" won victories in the year of the Emancipation centennial but sometimes the suffering was terrible to bear.

In April, William Moore, a white CORE member, began a "freedom walk" through the South. Walking along a highway in Alabama with a sign that said, "Equal Rights for All," he was killed by a sniper's bullet. In June, Medgar Evers, field secretary of the NAACP in Mississippi, a war veteran and the father of two, was shot in the back as he stepped from his car. He died an hour later.

In September, eighteen days after the March on Washington, black children were at Sunday school in the basement of the Sixteenth Street Baptist Church in Birmingham. The morning's lesson was "The Love That Forgives"—"Love your enemies, bless them that curse you . . ."

As the lesson ended a car drove along the street. It slowed down long enough for one of its occupants to toss a bomb at the church. The building's brick walls crumbled, rafters collapsed, stained-glass windows were shattered. And underneath the rubble lay the mangled bodies of four little girls.

"We give love—and we get this!" a boy screamed as he stood in the ruins.

"Love them? Love them?" another cried. "I hate them!"

The Iceberg

There was no time to mourn. In the summer of 1964 a nonviolent army moved into Mississippi. Since 1890, when its lawmakers led the South in disfranchising Negroes, black Mississippians had lived in poverty and fear, voteless and voiceless. Thousands were sharecroppers on the big plantations, picking cotton from sunup to sundown, their lives scarcely changed since slavery. James W. Silver, history professor at the University of Mississippi, called the state "a closed society" which "comes as close to a police state as anything we have yet seen

Sixteenth Street Baptist Church, Birmingham

in America." Robert Moses, a black New Yorker with a master's degree from Harvard, described it as "the middle of the iceberg" and made up his mild to melt it.

Moses came South in 1960, drawn by the student sit-ins. The following summer he gave up his job as a math teacher to join the staff of SNCC and set up a voter registration school in Mississippi. Black farmers, domestic workers, laborers came to school at night to study the 285 sections of the Mississippi constitution so they could pass the voter application tests. The studying was easy. The hard part came when the prospective voter went to the county courthouse and asked to register. Then would-be voters and the SNCC workers who accompanied them were threatened, beaten, jailed or killed.

Nevertheless the work went on. In 1962 there were seven voter registration projects in Mississippi. Only a handful of people actually registered but others caught a glimpse of the world outside their "closed society" and determined to join it. Fifteen-year-old Brenda Travis led a sit-in in a drugstore and was sentenced to a year in a reformatory. Forty-seven-year-old Fannie Lou Hamer lost her sharecropper's job and was evicted from her home the day she tried to register. Both became workers for SNCC. The Freedom Ballot campaign of 1963 brought hope to many more. At a meeting in a country church an old man smiled, "All these years, going along behind my plow, I thought some day things would change. But I never dreamed I'd see it."

In 1964 more than a thousand people went to Mississippi. Six hundred and fifty were youngsters, mostly college students, mostly white, who had volunteered to work in Freedom Schools and community centers and help black Mississippians register to vote. They were backed up by lawyers, doctors, nurses, ministers, who gave up a two-week vacation or a month's work to lend a hand. The Summer Project was organized by all the civil rights groups working in Mississippi—SNCC, CORE, SCLC and state branches of the NAACP—with Robert Moses as program director.

During a week of training on an Ohio campus, the volunteers were taught the facts of Mississippi life. "Fifty-one per cent of the people in the Delta earn less than a thousand dollars a year . . . Mississippi is not just a closed society. It's locked and the vote is the key that will open it . . . In Bolivar County the superintendent of schools forbids teaching foreign languages and civics in Negro schools—also American history from 1860 to 1875 . . . The schools are a kind of brain-washing. The Negro child is trained to accept without question. Teach him to ask why and the system will fail . . ."

"There's danger, real danger . . . Five Negroes were shot this winter . . . Some of you may lose your lives."

"It's hell in Mississippi!" Jimmy Travis, a tense twenty-two-year-old with bullet scars on his neck interrupted. "And you've got to realize that nobody cares. We care. They say that democracy exists in America. You have got to make it work in Mississippi so that it can work in the rest of the country."

"We're not thinking of integrating the lunch counters," Robert Moses explained. "Negroes in Mississippi haven't the money to eat in those places anyway. Your job is to strengthen local people. If you can go into Negro homes and just sit and talk, that will be a huge job. If each of you can leave behind three people who are stronger and more skilled than when you came, that will be three thousand more we'll have to work with next year."

Nonviolence was discussed more as a necessity than a philosophy. "If you carry guns or even pocketknives, the police can murder you and then claim self-defense." On the lawns of the campus the volunteers were shown how to "cover your head, roll up in a knot, hit the ground" when attacked. "If you're caught from behind go limp. If your friend is getting his head beat, fall on him, man! What happens to one happens to everybody."

These practice sessions took on an air of spine-chilling reality when Moses announced, "Three of our people are missing." Michael Schwerner, twenty-four, director of a community center

in Meridian, James Chaney, twenty-one, a CORE worker, and
Andrew Goodman, twenty, a volunteer who had been in the
state for only a day had driven to Neshoba County to investigate a church burning. Six weeks later FBI men found their
bodies buried under twenty feet of red Mississippi clay. The
prosecution of their murderers dragged on until December 1967.
Then seven men, including the deputy sheriff of Neshoba
County, were given jail sentences ranging from three to ten
years.

In Mississippi the volunteers became a part of the black
community, sharing the poverty of the poorest people in the
poorest state in the Union. At Freedom Schools, children heard
for the first time about Frederick Douglass, Harriet Tubman
and the Supreme Court ruling against segregated schools. Six-
year-olds told riddles:

> Q. *What has four eyes and can't see?*
> A. *Mississippi*

Twelve-year-olds wrote poems:

> *What is wrong with me?*
> *Everywhere I go*
> *No one seems to look at me.*
> *Sometimes I cry.*
>
> *I walk through the woods and sit on a stone.*
> *I look at the stars and I sometimes wish.*
> *Probably if my wish ever comes true,*
> *Everyone will look at me.*

Teen-agers held debates about violence versus nonviolence.
They saw plays and put on some of their own, re-enacting
the struggle in Birmingham or a trip to the courthouse to
register. After one Freedom School session, high schoolers decided to integrate the public library—which the city promptly
closed.

At the community centers older people learned to read, to
type, to paint pictures. They discussed taxes, how governments
were run, the different federal aid programs whose money sel-

dom reached Negro families.* At evening meetings they heard concerts and listened to speakers like Martin Luther King, entertainers like Sidney Poitier and Harry Belafonte.

Voter registration work moved more slowly. Fear kept people from going to the courthouse. Of those who went few were able to register. County registrars had absolute power to decide who passed or failed the voters' test. One persistent applicant was flunked ten times. On her eleventh try a congressman from New York who had come to Mississippi to see how the volunteers were faring accompanied her to the courthouse. That time she passed—the only Negro in her county to register in 1964. The congressman returned to Washington to work for a voters' rights law.

Unable to take part in the official election machinery of the state, Negroes founded the Freedom Democratic Party which was "open to all Democrats in Mississippi of voting age, regardless of race, creed, or color." Volunteers went from door to door and to churches and stores enrolling people as Freedom Democrats. Late in the summer the Freedom Party held county and state conventions. In halls decorated with banners proclaiming, ONE MAN—ONE VOTE and LBJ FOR PRESIDENT, black sharecroppers, teachers, housewives elected a slate of delegates to the National Democratic Convention.

At the convention, held in Atlantic City, New Jersey, during the last week in August, the Freedom Democrats challenged the right of the regular Democrats to their seats. Civil rights workers kept a round-the-clock vigil outside the convention hall, while Aaron Henry and Mrs. Fannie Lou Hamer told the Credentials Committee—and the millions who were watching television—of the oppression and terror that kept black citizens of Mississippi from the polls. Mrs. Hamer described a beating she had received in jail "till my hands were black and blue. Is this America?" she asked. "Is this the land of the free and the home of the brave?"

---

* The volunteers discovered that although Washington financed a school lunch program the money was going only to white schools.

Fannie Lou Hamer

The Democratic Party was shaken. A number of its leaders sided with the Freedom delegates. For two days the convention marked time as senators and congressmen tried to work out a compromise. The Freedom Democrats were offered two seats as delegates-at-large and a promise that things would be better by the time of the next national convention in '68. Although they turned down the offer, no one felt that the summer's work had been wasted.

Black Mississippi had been aroused from a long sleep. The Freedom Schools continued and a few youngsters braved hostile crowds to attend white schools in the fall. Women who had been fired for trying to register to vote formed co-operatives to make quilts and dresses. Farmers got together to learn how to get help from federal crop allotment programs. "It's not that people have lost their fear," a woman said, "but now they've got hope. With hope you can walk ahead with your fear."

The changes in white Mississippi were less striking. Moderates who spoke out were driven from the state while racists continued their campaign of terror. In addition to the three young men who were murdered, eighty Negro and white volunteers were beaten, three wounded by gunfire. More than a thousand were arrested on trumped-up charges and sixty-six Negro churches and homes were bombed or burned.

The iceberg had not melted but large cracks were appearing on its surface.

"It Is Wrong . . ."

While Freedom Democrats and student volunteers went on with their work in Mississippi, the national spotlight shifted to Selma, Alabama. Selma was Birmingham all over again, with Sheriff Jim Clark taking the place of "Bull" Connor. Most of Selma's Negro families lived on incomes well below $3000 a year—as against the national median income of $6249—and only 335 of them could vote.

Bombed church, Mississippi

In January 1965 SNCC, which had been trying to register voters in Selma, was joined by organizers for SCLC. "We are no longer fighting for a seat at the lunch counter," said Reverend James Bevel. "We're fighting for seats in the legislature. If we get out and work, Jim Clark will be picking cotton with my father in about two years."

The campaign built up slowly. At the end of the month the box score read: Arrests . . . 280, Registrations . . . o. In February, Martin Luther King led would-be registrants to the courthouse. He had recently returned from Europe where he had been awarded the Nobel Peace Prize, given annually to the person "who has done most for furtherance of brotherhood among men." In Selma he was thrown into jail.

After Dr. King's arrest long lines of people filled the courthouse square. Sheriff Clark and his men used night sticks and electrified cattle prods to drive them away. Hundreds, then thousands, were arrested. Released from jail, Dr. King proposed a march to the state capital at Montgomery to ask the legislature to end discrimination. When tear gas and clubs broke up this march and James Reeb, a white minister from Boston, was killed, men and women from all over the country flocked to Selma.

Black-garbed nuns came from California, priests from Chicago, ministers and rabbis from Detroit and New York . . . doctors, nurses, social workers, actors, folk singers, writers . . . civil rights leaders and black and white Alabamans. Carrying flags, singing, they marched along the highway. Congressmen's wives locked arms with housewives from Harlem. Trade union leaders walked with professors of American history. It rained, and they put boxes over their heads and improvised ponchos from sheets of plastic. At night they camped by the side of the road, nursing their blisters and sleeping in circus tents. At the end of the fifty-four-mile march they were twenty-five thousand strong.

In Montgomery, Governor George Wallace refused to meet with them but in Washington, President Johnson addressed a

Selma, Alabama, 1965

joint session of Congress to urge new voter legislation. "The
harsh fact is that in many places in this country men and
women are kept from voting simply because they are Negroes,"
he said. "It is wrong—deadly wrong—to deny any of your fellow
Americans the vote."

Four and a half months later he signed the Voting Rights
Act of 1965. All "understanding" tests were abolished and
federal examiners were authorized to register Negroes wherever local officials denied them the ballot. In 1966 more than
ten thousand Negroes registered in Selma. They went to the
polls and voted Sheriff Jim Clark out of office.

"THE HISTORY OF THE AMERICAN NEGRO
IS THE HISTORY OF . . . THIS LONGING
TO ATTAIN SELF-CONSCIOUS MANHOOD . . .
HE WOULD NOT AFRICANIZE AMERICA,
FOR AMERICA HAS TOO MUCH TO
TEACH THE WORLD AND AFRICA. HE WOULD
NOT BLEACH THE NEGRO SOUL IN A
FLOOD OF WHITE AMERICANISM, FOR HE
KNOWS THAT NEGRO BLOOD HAS A MESSAGE
FOR THE WORLD. HE SIMPLY WISHES TO
MAKE IT POSSIBLE FOR A MAN TO BE
BOTH A NEGRO AND AN AMERICAN WITHOUT
BEING CURSED AND SPIT UPON."

W. E. B. Du Bois, 1903

CHAPTER 18

Black Power

A March Against Fear

"I just wish there were some way to explain the awful fear that permeates the atmosphere for every Negro in this country, and especially the Negroes who inhabit the American South," James Meredith wrote. "I wish there were a way to explain what it is like to be a Negro moving down a deserted highway at night and see a car bearing strangers pulling out behind you. I wish I could put into words the sinking feeling in the stomach and the nervous twitching in the face which can come over a Negro when he confronts a southern sheriff."

After his graduation from the University of Mississippi, Meredith had studied in Africa and at Columbia law school in New York. But he still had unfinished business in his home state. To conquer this fear, for himself and other black Mississippians, he decided to walk across the state, alone, unarmed.

In June 1966 Meredith was on the second day of his "march against fear" when a white man stepped out from the bushes along the highway. He was cradling a shotgun in his arms.

"James Meredith," he called. "I want James Meredith."

As Meredith turned to face him, the man raised his gun. Three shots rang out. The Negro tumbled to the ground, a reddish stain slowly spreading across his shirt.

James Meredith

The shots failed to kill James Meredith. He awakened in a hospital room in Memphis the next morning to find the nation's civil rights leaders at his bedside. Before he left the hospital numbers of Negroes and whites had taken up his march and were following Highway 51 to Jackson, the state capital.

They walked for three weeks under the blazing Mississippi sun, visiting towns that had never seen a civil rights worker before. They were stoned in Philadelphia, Mississippi, and tear-gassed in Canton. In Sunflower County a woman waved them away.

"What you're doing now, some's going to get killed," she said. "In the North, there's something to hold the white man back. Here, there's nothing. He got all the jobs. You go to court, you can't ever win against him. He exercises the law the way he wants."

The march met its greatest success in Grenada where fear took a holiday for a few days. Just before the marchers reached town the "white" and "colored" signs in the courthouse were taken down and the segregated restaurants locked their doors. After a Negro dared to put an American flag on the Confederate monument in the town square, thirteen hundred black men and women lined up to register to vote. When the marchers left, the flag was replaced by the Stars and Bars of the Confederacy and teen-agers who tried to integrate the movie theater were jailed. Nevertheless, a Grenada Freedom Movement was formed and its members boycotted white businesses in an effort to win an "open city." In the fall their children were brutally attacked when they went, for the first time, to a "white" school.*

All told, the "march against fear" encouraged four thousand Mississippi Negroes to enroll as voters and thousands more began to stir. This was one more gain among the many that had been made in the struggle for full civil rights. But the shotgun blast that felled James Meredith and summoned hundreds

* See page 181.

to take his place also signalled the time when The Movement had to face a crucial question. With so much remaining to be won, could "soul power" really overcome the soulless fury of racism? Something more was needed, the young people of SNCC and CORE decided. Instead of marching to the slow rhythm of "We Shall Overcome," they swung along Highway 51 shouting, "BLACK POWER!"

What had happened to those neat polite college students who sat at lunch counters waiting patiently to be served? Where were the nonresisting Freedom Riders with their bloody heads and loving hearts?

The youngsters of 1960 were now veterans of a hundred battles. They had turned in their Ivy League suits for bib overalls. Instead of careful college diction they were talking the "down home" talk of the rural South or the hip talk of northern ghettos. Friends had been killed, homes and churches burned. They themselves carried the scars of club, shotgun and police dogs' teeth. They had seen a policeman kick a woman into semiconsciousness, shouting as he did so, "Nigger, you want your freedom? Well, here it is." They no longer had hope for "the beloved community." They no longer believed that love and suffering—*their* love, *their* suffering—would change the hearts of the segregationists. "From now on," they said, "Black Power!"

Bursting into the headlines, this new outcry startled most white Americans and some Negroes. For months the meaning of black power was debated on television and in the press. Sometimes patiently, sometimes angrily, its advocates tried to explain. "No, we're not anti-white. We're pro-Negro . . . Yes, we want white support but we think it's time black people took charge of their own organizations . . . No, we don't favor violence. The whites are the ones who are violent. But we are no longer going to tell Negroes not to defend themselves if they are attacked . . ."

"When we talk about black power everybody gets excited," complained Floyd McKissick, a North Carolina lawyer who replaced James Farmer as national director of CORE. "Two little bitty words in the English language. One—black—everybody that goes to the sixth grade knows what black means. Power— everybody that goes to the sixth grade knows what that means. And I get a letter from a professor at Harvard that says, 'Explain black power.'"

Black . . .

Two little bitty words, but when they were put together they spelled something old, something new. Despite the influence of a Frederick Douglass and a W. E. B. Du Bois, Negro Americans had been taught to have a poor opinion of themselves. Long before the sixth grade, children learned that the world was white and they were black. Other people had illustrious ancestors but the Africans in their social studies books were half-naked savages who had been conquered by white men. In the Bible they read that they were the sons of Ham, condemned by Noah's curse to be "a servant of servants." The dictionary told them that "black" meant evil while "white" stood for purity and goodness. Movie stars and beauty queens all had straight hair and light skin. Kinky hair was "bad" and had to be attacked with straightening combs and lotions to make it resemble the white ideal.

This negative picture began to change as Africans claimed Africa for themselves. Black ambassadors and prime ministers, handsome in their flowing robes, were speaking in the United Nations. The world, in fact, was not white but two thirds colored. Discovering African history, art, poetry American Negroes felt a new sense of their own worth. Even hair styles are changing as women reject white standards and begin to wear a natural "African look."

The Movement, too, gave Negroes a feeling of "somebodiness." "We've got to dig being black," a member of CORE told

Girl with African hair style

Stokely Carmichael

James Farmer. This was the message that Stokely Carmichael, newly elected chairman of SNCC, carried to Mississippi during the march. Carmichael had been a senior in a New York high school when the student sit-ins started. He made his first trip South as a Freedom Rider. After grimly unforgettable weeks in a Mississippi jail, he went to college during the winters and spent summers in Alabama and Mississippi with SNCC. He had grown to manhood in The Movement and the love in his heart was reserved for Negroes.

"It is time to stop being ashamed of being black," he told people along Highway 51. "When you see your daughter playing in the fields, with her nappy hair and her wide nose and her thick lips, tell her she is beautiful." With angry tenderness he repeated, *"Tell your daughter she is beautiful."*

BLACK IS BEAUTIFUL

AND IT'S SO BEAUTIFUL
TO BE BLACK

DR. MARTIN LUTHER KING, JR.
President, Southern Christian Leadership Conference
334 AUBURN AVENUE, N. E.
ATLANTA, GEORGIA, 30303

Malcolm X

The new-found pride in blackness was also a reflection of the growing strength of nationalist groups. Throughout history some Negroes had despaired of winning integration and had favored living apart—in Africa, the West Indies or in a section of the United States. After the Red Summer of 1919, Marcus Garvey, a black Jamaican, organized a million people into the Universal

Negro Improvement Association. With its slogan, "Africa for the Africans, at home and abroad," the UNIA backed Negro-owned businesses, Black Cross Nurses and a Black Star Steamship Line. Although his ships sank and Garvey himself went to jail, his ideas came to the fore again with the growth of the Black Muslims.

A religious rather than a civil rights group, the Muslims reject Christianity and believe that American Negroes are the fabled Lost Nation of Islam, soon to be restored by Allah to their rightful place in the world. They preach black supremacy and a hatred of whites, "the blue-eyed devils" who enslaved Negroes and robbed them of their names and true religion. To them, the solution to the race problem is separation, and they ask for a portion of the United States, perhaps nine or ten states, where they can live and rule themselves.

The Muslims are more than a Sunday religion. Their strict moral code forbids alcohol, tobacco, gambling, and puts great stress on cleanliness, thrift and self-reliance. Muslim men and women dress conservatively and, as far as possible, operate their own bakeries, barbershops, restaurants. In the big-city ghettos where most Muslims live, they have had extraordinary success in reforming criminals and dope addicts and giving the poor and the undereducated a new self-respect and purpose in life.

Although the Black Muslims are headed by the Honorable Elijah Muhammad, their most effective spokesman was, for many years, a fiercely proud and brainy man who called himself Malcolm X. He had been born Malcolm Little but in accordance with Muslim doctrine had dropped his last name* because it was the name given to his ancestors when they were slaves. He said what few Negroes dared to say but most believed— that the white man was guilty of a thousand crimes against the Negro, "and the worst crime has been to teach us to hate ourselves." Although the Muslim philosophy of hate instead of

* Some Muslims are granted an entirely new name. Thus Cassius Clay, winner of the world heavyweight boxing championship, has rejected his former name and is now called Muhammad Ali.

love, separation instead of integration, opposed everything the civil rights movement stood for, Malcolm's slashing attacks on whites and his message of self-esteem had a considerable impact on Negro thought.

"He would make you angry as hell," said actor Ossie Davis, "but he would also make you proud. And you always left his presence with the sneaky suspicion that maybe, after all, you *were* a man!"

As he traveled across the United States and abroad, speaking to different kinds of people, Malcolm's ideas changed. In 1964 he broke with the Black Muslims. Convinced that their separate state was an impractical dream, he started the Organization of Afro-American Unity to fight for Negro rights. Although he limited his organization to blacks, he no longer considered all white men as "devils." Instead, he proposed that those who sincerely wanted to solve the race problem go to work "where America's racism really is—among their fellow whites." His message scarcely had time to sink in when, in February 1965, he was assassinated. In death Malcolm became a legend—"our black shining Prince"—whose influence spreads in widening circles from northern ghettos to the weather-beaten shanties of the South.

. . . Power

When the militant young people of SNCC and CORE defined power they talked first about Lowndes County, Alabama, where two white civil rights workers had been killed after the Selma march. "Bloody Lowndes," as it was nicknamed, had a population of 15,417 people. More than 12,000 were Negroes, but 86 white families owned nine tenths of the land. The black men and women of Lowndes County earned a median income of $935 a year and lived in shacks without running water and bathtubs. Almost all of the white babies of Lowndes County were born in hospitals. But 91 per cent of the Negro babies were born at home—the highest rate in the nation.

No Negro had voted in Lowndes County since reconstruction. The sheriff was white. The tax assessor and tax collector were white and so were the members of the school board.

This, said The Movement spokesmen, was powerlessness.

After the Voters Rights Act was passed, a federal registrar came to Lowndes County. Black people saw their first hope of a change. In a few weeks, 2681 Negroes registered. Then the question arose—for whom should they vote? The Republican

White Sheriff and black voters

Party was almost nonexistent in the county. The leading Democrats were the same men who had blocked the courthouse steps when Negroes had tried to register before. With SNCC's help, the Negroes formed a third party, the Lowndes County Freedom Party, and nominated their own candidates for office.

Alabama's election law requires political parties to have an emblem as well as a name. The Republican's emblem is an elephant. The state Democrats' emblem is a white rooster which, until the slogan was removed in 1966, crowed, "WHITE SUPREMACY." For their emblem the Freedom Party chose a black panther, or mountain lion, an animal that is still seen occasionally in the backwoods of Alabama. "The panther moves back until it is cornered," said John Hulett, chairman of the new party. "Then it comes out fighting for life or death. We felt that the panther could destroy the rooster."

During the summer and fall of 1966, members of the Freedom Party traveled through Lowndes County, holding meetings and explaining, with primers which they wrote themselves, what it would mean if their candidates were elected. A black sheriff could keep law and order in a county famous for its lawlessness. A black tax assessor could raise the taxes on the big plantations and channel funds for the building of better roads and schools. Black school board members could see that the black schools, that then had sixty pupils in a class, became as good as the white schools.

"Once we take over the county government, instead of having two communities, white and black, we will have one community, where people could sit down and talk across the table with one another," Hulett said. "This is what we're working for."

But the white people had economic power. In the weeks before election, sharecropper families were evicted from plantations on which they had lived most of their lives. Domestic workers, factory employees, bricklayers were fired. On Election Day, planters drove their field hands to the polls in the back of pickup trucks and watched closely to see that they did not

IS THIS THE PARTY YOU WANT?

DEMOCRATIC PARTY

OF ALABAMA

or

IS THIS ?

LOWNDES COUNTY FREEDOM ORGANIZATION

ONE MAN -- ONE VOTE

speak to the Freedom organizers. Although Negroes outnumbered whites on the voting rolls, the Freedom Party candidates lost the election.

The struggle for power in Lowndes County is still going on. Negroes have gotten together to buy land and build homes for some of the evicted families. They are raising money for a co-operative business to give work to some of the men and women who lost their jobs. There will be other elections and some day they will win.

The lesson of Lowndes County, said the supporters of black power, could be repeated wherever large numbers of Negroes lived. As the Irish had done in Boston and the Germans in Milwaukee, Negroes must work together to elect men to office who would work for them.

For years The Movement had been speaking from a position of weakness, Stokely Carmichael explained. It had been saying, "Look, man, it's morally wrong for you to treat us this way. We're marching and getting beat up. You should be ashamed of yourself." Now it planned to speak from strength. "*We* pick the candidate and make sure he fulfills our needs. Black Power doesn't mean anti-white, violence, or separatism. It's saying, 'Look, buddy, we represent X number of votes. We're not laying a vote on you unless you lay so many schools, hospitals, playgrounds and jobs on us.'"

"WHAT HAPPENS TO A DREAM DEFERRED?
DOES IT DRY UP
LIKE A RAISIN IN THE SUN?
OR FESTER LIKE A SORE—
AND THEN RUN?
MAYBE IT JUST SAGS
LIKE A HEAVY LOAD.
OR DOES IT EXPLODE?"

Langston Hughes

CHAPTER 19

The End of the Beginning

The Widening Gulf

Twelve years after Rosa Parks said "no" to the bus driver, Jim Crow was legally dead. Supreme Court decisions and acts of Congress had outlawed segregation. In Montgomery where it all started, restaurants, hotels, parks were open to everyone. The bus station had only one waiting room and some Negro youngsters attended the Robert E. Lee High School.

Millions of Negroes were voting in the South. Black men were elected to the legislatures of Mississippi, Georgia, Tennessee and Texas. Three Mississippi counties had black justices of the peace and Macon County, Alabama, had a black sheriff for the first time since reconstruction.

Ralph Bunche, grandson of a slave, was still United Nations Undersecretary for Special Political Affairs. Robert Weaver was Secretary of Housing and Urban Development, the first Negro in the U. S. Cabinet, and Thurgood Marshall was a justice of the Supreme Court. Brown-skinned Edward Brooke represented the state of Massachusetts in the U. S. Senate, and

there were six Negroes in the House of Representatives.*
Walter Washington, Commissioner of the District of Columbia,
and Carl Stokes, Mayor of Cleveland, were the first Negro
chief executives of major American cities. Ten federal judges
and six ambassadors were Negroes. So were the postmasters
of New York, Chicago, and Los Angeles.

Negro actors were playing more important roles more fre-
quently on television. Books by Negro writers were best sellers.
Ivy League colleges were seeking out Negro students and
business was hiring them after graduation.

Yet in 1964 Negroes poured into the streets of New York
to throw bottles and bricks at the police, overturn cars, loot
stores. In 1965 riots erupted in Rochester, Philadelphia, and
the Watts section of Los Angeles. The "long hot summers"
that followed saw the flames of Negro revolt leap from city
to city. There were uprisings in Chicago, Cleveland, San
Francisco, in Newark, New Jersey, and Detroit, Michigan.
In Detroit whole city blocks were burned to the ground and
scores of people, most of them black, lost their lives.

Unlike the Red Summer of 1919, these were not race riots
with white and black pitted against each other. Although the
rioters shouted, "Get Whitey!" they did not move into areas
where whites lived. Instead they smashed and burned their
own neighborhoods in a hopeless, despairing rage, as if to say,
"For the last time, look, listen!"

"For years we've been trying to get the mayor to come out
and talk to us but he wouldn't come," a man said after the
explosion in Watts in which thirty-four people—thirty of them
Negroes—lost their lives and forty million dollars' worth of
property was destroyed. "For years we tried to get the governor
but he wouldn't come. For years we tried to get all those white
folks downtown to come and pay some attention to us. But
after we burned, baby, the whole world came to look at us."

Angry young spokesmen for "black power" described the
outbreaks as "dress rehearsals for revolution." H. Rap Brown,

* But in 1875 there were seven Negro congressmen and one Negro senator.

successor to Stokely Carmichael as chairman of SNCC, called on Negroes to celebrate August 18, 1965, as the beginning of their struggle for independence. "That day marks the day the blacks of Watts picked up guns to fight for their freedom," he said. "That was our Declaration of Independence."

Whether the outbreaks are spoken of as "riots" or "rebellions," their message is plain, for those who care to listen. In spite of civil rights laws, the day-to-day life of most black Americans has not improved. The gulf between the Negro and the rest of American society has been widening.

"The Negro baby born in America today," President Kennedy said in 1963, "has about one-half as much chance of completing high school as a white baby born on the same day— one-third as much chance of completing college—one-third as much chance of becoming a professional man—twice as much chance of becoming unemployed—about one-seventh as much chance of earning $10,000 per year—a life expectancy which is seven years less—and the prospects of earning only half as much."

The statistics have scarcely changed since then. The Negro unemployment rate remains twice as high as that of whites. In some areas—Watts is one of them—30 per cent of the men are without work. In all areas, 27 per cent of Negro teen-agers are jobless, as compared with a 12 per cent unemployment figure for white youth.

"A Negro ain't got a chance in this world," a boy in Oakland, California, said. "You go to high school, man, and you still can't get a job. There ain't no sense in studying."

"Are you looking for a job?" Secretary of Labor W. Willard Wirtz asked a young man on a street corner in Harlem. "Why?" was the hopeless reply.

Most Negroes who are employed have the lowest-paying, least-skilled jobs. In Cleveland, where Negroes make up 13 per cent of the population, they hold only 3.2 per cent of the white collar jobs. Negroes in Chicago occupy 4.7 per cent of the white collar jobs, in Kansas City, 2.1 per cent. The situation

Street corner, Watts

is even worse in southern cities like Atlanta and New Orleans. In New Orleans Negroes make up 30.7 per cent of the population but hold 3 per cent of the white collar jobs.

"The basement doors have been opened," Secretary Wirtz said, "but the doors on the stairs are still locked."

Although the Civil Rights Act of 1964 forbids discrimination in hiring and promotions, the Equal Employment Opportunity Commission set up by the act has no enforcement powers. A man who has been discriminated against must take his own case to court. The NAACP has already filed complaints of job bias against almost two thousand employers, many of them the biggest businesses in the land.

The record of unions, particularly in the building trades, is not much better. In Cleveland where a quarter of a million Negroes live, only five have been accepted in union apprentice programs. Cincinnati building unions have twenty-one Negro apprentices out of a total of four hundred and fifty. In Watts some construction unions have no Negro members at all.

In a time of growing prosperity, the median yearly incomes of Negro families across the United States is $3971. For white families it is $7170. Since World War II, the number of white families living in poverty has decreased by 27 per cent while the number of poor Negro families decreased by 3 per cent.

Prices in the ghetto are higher than in other parts of the city. Negroes get less value for their rent dollars and pay more for food. A survey of drugstores in New York showed that medicines cost more in Harlem than in white neighborhoods.

In the ghetto, prices are high but life is cheap. Most riots have been triggered by incidents involving the police. Harlem exploded after an off-duty policeman shot and killed a fifteen-year-old boy. The death of another teen-ager—shot in the back by a policeman who suspected him of car stealing—touched off a riot in San Francisco. Chicago Negroes thronged into the streets when a policeman clubbed a boy who had turned on a fire hydrant on a muggy summer day.

Although most Americans look to the police for protection, many Negroes fear and distrust them, according to the President's national crime commission. The commission's observers report that policemen on their beats issue "brusque or nasty" commands to Negroes and sometimes rough them up in the station house. At the White House Conference on Civil Rights held in 1966 a spokesman for a northern city said, "I'm sorry to point out that some people think of the police as an occupying army, an enemy." Charges of police brutality were so wide-

"A guy's entitled to a jury of his peers, ain't he?"

spread that the Conference recommended the establishment of civilian review boards to investigate them.

The ghettos are growing larger. With mechanical cotton pickers and chemical weed killers taking the place of hand labor on southern plantations, two million Negroes have migrated to northern and western cities since 1960. Home building has not kept pace with the arrival of the newcomers. Of all new housing built since World War II less than 2 per cent has gone to black families. Buildings that were old and crowded are now older and more crowded. "There are nine in my family and we live in a one-and-a-half room apartment," said a letter in the New York *Amsterdam News*. "We are working people who wish only to have a decent home for our children, but we just don't know what to do any more."

The U. S. Civil Rights Commission reports that "housing discrimination is perhaps the most deeply rooted civil rights problem in America." A national law to forbid discrimination failed to pass Congress in 1967. Twenty-one states and more than forty-five cities have open housing laws, but they work rather feebly. A Negro who sees a VACANCY sign in an apartment outside the ghetto is likely to be told, "So sorry. We just rented the apartment to another family." It is then up to him to prove to the State Human Rights Commission that this is untrue. Sometimes, after months of hearings, he wins his case only to have the landlord repeat, "So sorry. I sold the building last week. The new owner has rented the apartment to someone else."

In New York the Urban League has a program called Operation Open City. When a Negro looks for an apartment he is followed by a white volunteer who checks to see if the apartment has really been rented. If the landlord has lied, the "checker" testifies to this effect. Even with such help, Operation Open City has been able to find apartments for only 10 per cent of the people who apply.

The two million newcomers and the millions who came before them must live someplace, so the ghetto expands, street by street. Whites living along its borders move to the suburbs where they do not have to face the problems of urban crowding and urban poverty. "There is an ever-increasing concentration of nonwhites in the decaying centers of our cities," says the U. S. Civil Rights Commission, "while a 'white noose' of new suburban housing grows up around them."

Negroes and whites live apart. They work at different kinds of jobs and they go to separate schools. While the South has been inching along toward desegregation, *de facto* segregation has increased in the North. Ten years ago New York had sixty-four schools that were almost all Negro and Puerto Rican. Today the number of such schools has more than doubled.

Across the continent in an Atlanta, Georgia, slum, a black woman said, "From here we can see the banks and the tall apartment buildings in the white area of the city. We can see the universities and the big wide clean streets. No one comes to see us."

The Seamless Web

What can be done?

If the ghetto walls were to come down tomorrow and Negroes were welcomed in "white" neighborhoods, many would not have the money to buy or rent homes. They need jobs and better jobs.

If employers and unions suddenly became "color-blind," many Negroes would not be able to qualify for better jobs because they lack the necessary skills. They need better education.

Segregated schools are failing to prepare children for today's world of computers and electronic machines. But you cannot get rid of segregated schools unless you get rid of segregated neighborhoods. And you cannot get rid of segregated neighborhoods until you have equal employment opportunities. And you cannot have that unless you provide an equal education.

President Johnson has described the situation as "a seamless web." "You do not wipe away the scars of centuries by saying: Now, you are free to go where you want," he said. "You do not take a man who, for years, has been hobbled by chains, liberate him, bring him up to the starting line of a race, and then say, 'You're free to compete with all the others.' It is not enough just to open the gates of opportunity.

"The task is to give twenty million Negroes the same chance

as every other American to learn and grow, to work and share in society, to develop their abilities—physical, mental, and spiritual—and to pursue their individual happiness."

The National Urban League has proposed a "more-than-equal" program in which employers would seek out qualified Negroes for jobs and would step up training programs to prepare new Negro employees and upgrade those already employed. "For more than three hundred years," says Whitney Young, the Urban League's executive director, "the white American has received 'preferential treatment' over the Negro. What we ask now is that there be a deliberate and massive effort to include the Negro citizen in the mainstream of American life. We are not asking for equal time. A major effort, honestly applied, need last only ten years."

Dr. Martin Luther King, Jr., asked the United States to spend ten billion dollars a year in the next ten years to get rid of the conditions that cause Negro riots and unrest. "It is much more important to put men on their own two feet on earth than to put men on the moon," he said.

A. Philip Randolph has prepared a $185 billion* "Freedom Budget" to end poverty in the United States by 1975. His Budget calls for government and private spending to create enough jobs to end unemployment, the building of seventeen million new homes and the investment of large sums in education, health services and care for the aged. The Freedom Budget, which is backed by civil rights, labor and religious leaders would benefit all those with low incomes, whites as well as Negroes.

Dr. Kenneth Clark, the psychologist whose testimony on the damage caused by segregation helped shape the Supreme Court's decision in 1954, believes that superior schools in the ghettos are a first step to break through "the seamless web." Pessimistic about the possibility of ending *de facto* segregation in the near future, he recommends the transformation of ghetto

* $185 billion spent over an eight-year period can be compared with the $74 billion spent for national defense in a single year.

schools, from prekindergarten upward, "to save as many Negro children as possible now." When whites flee to the suburbs to escape from schools in which the proportion of Negroes is increasing, "the quality of the schools does indeed decline," he explains, "*not* because Negroes are inferior, but because the school system behaves as though they are." Once these schools become top rated, white children will return to them. "The goals of integration and quality education are interdependent," Dr. Clark says. "One is not possible without the other."

Floyd McKissick of CORE is asking for "many millions" of dollars for self-help programs that would "transfer power from whites to blacks" in fourteen cities where Negroes will have voting majorities in a few years' time. In addition to better schools, the programs would stress participation in politics, leadership training, consumer co-operatives, and the building of a positive self-image. "White people want black people to say they're Americans and to forget their ties to Africa," McKissick explains. "But on Sunday there was an Israeli festival in Central Park and a Polish-American parade on Fifth Avenue. The Germans march on Steuben Day and the Chinese-Americans celebrate their own New Year and the Italian-Americans let out a big yell when somebody said a Viking beat Columbus to America. The black man here has an 'identity gap' that has led in many cases to self-hatred."

Bits and pieces of these proposals are being put into effect by federal antipoverty programs and local boards of education. Some integrated housing is being built. Some college students are spending their summers tutoring ghetto children. The Urban League has set up skills banks and on-the-job training programs to help Negroes get better jobs. Thousands have found work as receptionists, bank tellers, lab technicians, engineers, but millions more need help.

The Unfinished Revolution

In the South, almost three million Negroes have registered to vote—and more than two million are not yet registered. Sixteen per cent of the Negro boys and girls go to schools with white children—and 84 per cent attend inferior, all-black schools. In Mississippi, Louisiana and Alabama fewer than five out of every hundred Negroes go to "white" schools. The South has seen more than ninety Negro and civil rights workers murdered since 1954. In only five instances have their killers received jail sentences.

The NAACP is still fighting in all fifty states to see that the promise of freedom becomes a reality. In a single year its Legal Defense Fund lawyers defended fourteen thousand individuals who were victims of discrimination and brought three hundred and seventy-five civil rights cases to the courts. On Long Island, NAACP members demanded the right to join a volunteer fire department. In Milwaukee they fight for open housing. In Ohio and in New Rochelle, New York, they picket construction sites where building unions refuse to accept Negro members. In Mississippi they struggle to register voters and desegregate the schools. In Washington they lobby for a civil rights act that will really stop housing discrimination and give the government greater power to prosecute the murderers of civil rights workers.

The Southern Christian Leadership Conference and its affiliates still carry on voter registration drives and citizenship education programs in the South. The Montgomery Improvement Association wins new retail jobs. The Alabama Christian Movement stages "mourning marches" in Birmingham to protest police brutality. The Grenada, Mississippi Freedom Movement fights for protection for the black children attending "white" schools. But there are also Cleveland and Chicago Freedom Movements and Dr. Martin Luther King led marches into lily-white suburbs and helped organize rent strikes in slum tenements. "Our movement isn't over," Dr. King said. "Some of us are going to have to pack our bags and make our way to Washington, to make known to the President and every member of the Cabinet that we are here to stay, until something is done about our plight."

CORE still has chapters in southern states, but it has moved its national office from downtown New York to Harlem and its "target cities" are Baltimore, Cleveland, and Los Angeles. In addition to organizing black voters, working for better housing and jobs, its program now calls for the teaching of an African language in ghetto schools and the development of black art and cultural centers in ghetto communities.

Fanning out from their headquarters in Atlanta, SNCC's field workers are building "freedom organizations" in the black counties of Alabama, Mississippi, Georgia and in Phillips County, Arkansas, where men still remember the sharecroppers of Elaine. But they are also organizing in Watts, Harlem, Detroit, and in the black city of Washington, D.C., where Negroes are in the majority but cannot vote in local elections.*

The leaders of SCLC, SNCC, and CORE are opposed to the war in Vietnam. They believe that the war is wrong and that the billions being spent for armaments could be better used to build houses in the slums and improve the ghetto schools. Thus, for the first time since the Mexican War of 1846, the civil rights struggle has become directly tied to an important issue of the nation's foreign policy.

Although Dr. King did not lose his faith in the power of nonviolent direct action, The Movement has shifted its emphasis from mass demonstrations to political organizing. In the North the Negro vote has long been controlled by big-city machines whose candidates make promises that are seldom kept after Election Day. By banding together, Negroes are beginning to influence city school boards and win a voice in

* Since reconstruction all citizens of Washington have been deprived of the vote. The District of Columbia is governed by Congress, through Senate and House district committees. Washingtonians voted in a national election for the first time in 1964. They are still fighting for a home-rule bill that will permit them to chose their own mayor and city government.

antipoverty programs. In Chicago, which has a black population of a million, a newly formed Independent Political Organization bucked the machine to elect two independents to the City Council in 1967. "We have come to realize," said one of the councilmen, "that the social injustice suffered by the black man in America will be remedied only by seizing the political power that has been denied us so long."

Black voters can bring about changes in city councils and in the Congress of the United States, where they are still under-represented. Whether they will be able to destroy the core of racism that exists in white America remains to be seen.

In the spring of 1967 the city of Birmingham held the concluding event of its festival of the arts in the Sixteenth Street Baptist Church, which had been bombed four years earlier. The church has been rebuilt with contributions from all over the world. A stained-glass window sent by the people of Wales shows Jesus on the cross, with the words, "You Do It to Me." As an integrated audience listened to the singing of an integrated choir, more than one person recalled the words of a white Birmingham lawyer, the day after the four girls were killed:

"Who threw that bomb? We all did it. The 'who' is every individual who spreads the seeds of hate to his neighbor and his son. It is every senator and every representative who in the halls of Congress tells the world that things back home aren't really like they are. It is courts that move ever so slowly and newspapers that timorously defend the law. It is all the Christians and all the ministers who spoke too late."

Every white American shares responsibility for "the seamless web" that hobbles the feet and binds the hands of twenty million black citizens . . . the Mississippians who beat children with chains and the New Yorkers who protest against bussing their children out of their neighborhoods . . . the Lowndes County plantation owner and the Los Angeles businessman who turns down a Negro applicant for a job . . . the Southerners who kept silent and the Northerners who moved to the sub-

"What Do You Mean, 'Not So Fast'?"

urbs . . . those who say, "Never!" and those who say, "Today, but not next door!" . . . the Klansmen and the slum landlords . . . the church bombers and the churchgoers . . . the thoughtless, the uninformed and the unconcerned.

There are white as well as black poor in the South. In one or two communities The Movement has stirred them into action. A white Mississippi farmer who has joined forces with his black neighbors to fight for Head Start and other antipoverty programs tells a story:

A colored man was hauling a big timber to the sawmill with six big horses. He got stuck in the mud. A white man with a small cart, drawn by two small ponies, passed by on his way to town to get commodities.

"Looks like you got trouble there," the white man said. "Yes, sir," the colored man said. "Well, I'd help you if you wasn't a nigger," the white man said and drove off.

Well, the colored man got free and took his log to the mill. The white man loaded his buggy down with groceries and was on his way home, and his two ponies couldn't carry the load, and he got stuck.

The colored man came by and saw the white man and said, "Looks like you got trouble there." "Yes," the white man said. "Well, hell," the colored man said, "that little load ain't nothing for my big horses. Let's transfer to my wagon."

They did and when they got the load to the white man's house the man said, "Well, I sure thank you. Is there anything I can do for you? Can I give you some money or some food?"

"No," the colored man said.

"Well, I'd sure like to do something for you."

"There is one thing," the colored man said.

"What's that?"

"You got a son, don't you?"

"Yes."

"Well, if you want to do something for me, go raise that boy up different from what your daddy raised you."

On April 4, 1968, as this book went to press,
Dr. Martin Luther King was killed by an assas-
sin in Memphis, Tennessee.

Suggested Reading

Aptheker, Herbert. A DOCUMENTARY HISTORY OF THE NEGRO
  PEOPLE IN THE UNITED STATES. Citadel. 1951.
Bennett, Lerone. BEFORE THE MAYFLOWER. Penguin. 1966.
Bontemps, Arna, and Conroy, Jack. ANYPLACE BUT HERE. Hill
  and Wang. 1966.
Buckmaster, Henrietta. LET MY PEOPLE GO. Beacon. 1959.

Farmer, James. FREEDOM—WHEN? Random House. 1965.

Franklin, John Hope. FROM SLAVERY TO FREEDOM. Knopf. 1956.

Hansberry, Lorraine. THE MOVEMENT. Simon and Schuster. 1964.

Hughes, Langston. FIGHT FOR FREEDOM, The Story of the NAACP. Berkeley. 1962.

Kennedy, John F. A NATION OF IMMIGRANTS. Harper and Row. 1964.

King, Jr., Martin Luther. STRIDE TOWARD FREEDOM. Ballantine. 1960.

———. WHY WE CAN'T WAIT. New American Library. 1964.

Lewis, Anthony, and the New York *Times*. PORTRAIT OF A DECADE. Bantam. 1965.

Litwack, Leon F. NORTH OF SLAVERY. University of Chicago. 1965.

Malcolm X and Haley, Alex. THE AUTOBIOGRAPHY OF MALCOLM X. Grove. 1966.

Mannix, Daniel P. and Cowley, Malcolm. BLACK CARGOES. Viking. 1965.

Meltzer, Milton. IN THEIR OWN WORDS. 3 vols. Crowell. 1964–7.

Osofsky, Gilbert. HARLEM: THE MAKING OF A GHETTO. Harper and Row. 1966.

Peck, James. FREEDOM RIDE. Grove. 1962.

Quarles, Benjamin. THE NEGRO IN THE MAKING OF AMERICA. Collier. 1964.

Stampp, Kenneth M. THE ERA OF RECONSTRUCTION. Knopf. 1965.

Sterling, Dorothy. FOREVER FREE. Doubleday. 1963.

Sutherland, Elizabeth, ed. LETTERS FROM MISSISSIPPI. New American Library. 1965.

Woodward, C. Vann. THE STRANGE CAREER OF JIM CROW. Oxford. 1966.

Young, Whitney. TO BE EQUAL. McGraw-Hill. 1964.

Zinn, Howard. SNCC: THE NEW ABOLITIONISTS. Beacon. 1964.

Illustration Credits

Page 156. From the U. S. Army

CHAPTER 14

Page 163. From *The Crisis*

Pages 165, 168. From Wide World

CHAPTER 15

Pages 172, 177, 180, 183. From Wide World

Page 175. Photo from UPI

CHAPTER 16

Pages 188, 191, 197, 199. From Wide World

CHAPTER 17

Pages 203, 204, 207, 219. From Wide World

Page 210. Photo by Danny Lyons

Page 215. Photo by Cliff Vaughs for SNCC

Page 217. Photo by Francis Mitchell for SNCC

CHAPTER 18

Page 221. From Wide World

Page 225. Photo by Joffre Clark for SNCC

Page 226. Photo by Charmian Chaplan for SNCC

Page 227. From the Southern Christian Leadership Conference

Page 228. Photo by Francis Mitchell for SNCC

Page 231. Southern Patriot photo

Page 233. Lowndes County Freedom Organization

CHAPTER 19

Page 238. From Wide World

Page 244. From the National Urban League

Index

Dorothy Sterling is a native New Yorker who lives in Rye, New York, with her husband. She was educated at Wellesley and Barnard Colleges and worked at Time, Inc., before leaving to devote herself to her family and her writing.

Mrs. Sterling has been active in civil rights groups for almost twenty years. In addition to serving on the boards of the Rye-Port Chester branch of the NAACP and the Westchester Urban League, she has been a supporter of the Congress of Racial Equality and the Student Nonviolent Co-ordinating Committee. She was a founding member of the Rye Council for Human Rights. Among her other books are many on the natural sciences and such titles relating to Negro history and life as *Mary Jane, Freedom Train: Story of Harriet Tubman,* and *Captain of the Planter: Story of Robert Smalls.*